「英語サンドイッチメソッド」とは

デイビッド・セイン式英語学習法「英語サンドイッチメソッド」を世に出して、読者のみなさまから「はじめて毎日続けられた！」「英語が楽しく聞けるようになった」など、喜びの声をたくさんいただきました。そしてさらに「ぜひ第2弾を出してほしい」「次は日常会話編がほしい」などの多くの要望が寄せられました。

そこで、作られたのがこの本です。
この本では、レストランや駅、ホテルの他、TV番組や観光といった様々なシチュエーションでの日常会話を扱っています。海外旅行や海外出張、ホームステイはもちろん、日本国内で英語が必要になったときにもきっと役立つことでしょう。

第1弾を読まなくても大丈夫！ この本から始めてOKです！
ぜひこの本で、大好評の英語学習法「英語サンドイッチメソッド」を体験して、英会話力アップを目指してください！
第1弾をすでに終えた方は、さらなる日常会話力アップのために、この第2弾も聞いてみてください。

Introduction

英語が話せる
ようになるには、
まず
「聞く力」
をつけることが大切です。

こんなことありませんか？

海外旅行で
外国人に道を聞いたのだけど、
何を言っているのか
わからなかった…

外国のレストランで、
ウェイターさんに
どんな料理か聞いたのだけど、
何を言っているのか
わからなかった…

Introduction

会話の基本は
キャッチボールです。

それは、**英語も日本語も同じ**。

相手の言っていることがわからないと
会話のキャッチボールはできないので、
英語がうまく話せるようになりません。

さらに、
漢字など、文字の形に意味があるために
「目から覚える」と効率が良いといわれる
日本語と違い、
英語は音声が重視されるので
「耳から覚える」と効率が良い
といわれています。

そのため、英語を習得するには、
とにかく英語を聞いて
耳から理解できるようになることが
とても大切です。

「英語サンドイッチメソッド」は
CDを聞くだけ!
英語を聞き取りキャッチする力を
身につけることができます。

Introduction

英語サンドイッチメソッドのすごいところは次の**3点**です!

> Point **1**　CDを聞くだけ!
> Point **2**　ネイティブの頭の中を再現
> Point **3**　1日3分から始められる!

Point 1
CDを聞くだけ！

英語で会話をするには、
相手が何を言っているのか
理解することからスタートしないといけません。
さらに、英語は「耳から覚える言葉」といわれており、
聞くことが特に重視されます。

「英語サンドイッチメソッド」は、CDを聞くだけ！
英語を聞き取る力を身につけることができます。

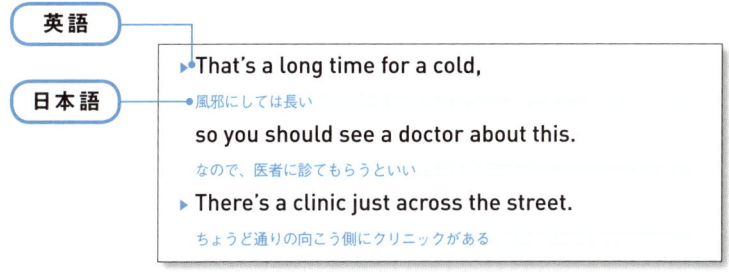

Introduction

Point 2
ネイティブの頭の中を再現

ネイティブは英語を、文章でもなく、
単語の組み合わせでもなく、
「意味のかたまり」で考えています。

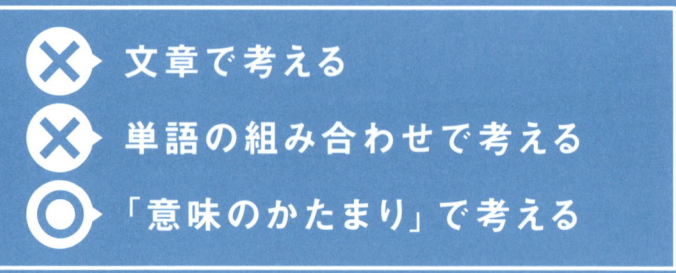

「英語サンドイッチメソッド」を聞くと、
この感覚が身についてきます。
文章が「意味のかたまり」で区切られていると、
違和感があり、聞き流せないので、
英語がしっかり頭に入ります。

Point 3
1日3分から始められる！

1日3分から始められるので、
忙しい人でも
無理なく続けられます。

継続は英語力アップのポイントなので、
毎日続けて聞くことをおすすめします。

もちろん、
1日3分以上くり返し聞いてもOK！
たくさん聞けば聞いた分だけ、
より早く効果を実感することができるでしょう。

Introduction

こんなに簡単にできる
「英語サンドイッチメソッド」。
ぜひこんな時に聞いてください。

電車の中で

車の中で

料理をしながら

洗濯物をたたみながら

お風呂で

英語サンドイッチメソッドの使い方

1日3分〜CDを聞くだけ!

1日1例文、CDを聞くことから始めましょう。さらに「もっと聞きたい!」という人は、何度でも繰り返し聞いてもOK。いつでもどこでもあなたの好きなときに聞いてください。

ネイティブの話すナチュラルスピードで、意味のかたまりごとに英語と日本語訳が読まれるので、音声を聞くだけで英語の内容が分かります。

テキストはCDを聞いた後に復習用に使うのがおすすめです。

※テキストのタイトル番号が、そのままトラック番号になります。CDの総再生時間は67分です。
※本書のCDは、CDプレーヤーでご使用ください。パソコンなどでの使用の際、再生できない場合があります。
※ディスクはキズや汚れがつかないように注意してください。
　また、ディスクが破損したり、故障した場合、無理に補修したり、そのままプレーヤーで使用するのは避けてください。

英語をさらに深く理解したい人はテキストを利用してください

1 通し英文と日本語訳で全体像を確認

通しの英文で、英文の全体像をつかみましょう。また、通しの日本語訳もついているので、自然な日本語で英文の内容を確認でき、復習にピッタリです。

2 英語の意味のかたまりを目で見て確認

CDに収録されている、英語と日本語のサンドイッチ構造の音声がそのまま掲載されています。英語の意味のかたまりを目で確認して、ネイティブが英語を話すときの感覚を養いましょう。リスニングの確認にもおすすめです。

3 押さえておきたい英単語をチェック

それぞれの英文の中で覚えておきたい単語をキーワードとして抜き出してあります。これらの単語を覚えておくと、実際に英語を話すときにとても便利です。

4 難しい例文や表現もスッキリ

分かりにくい英文や表現を詳しく解説します。英語を聞いたり話したりするときの、ポイントになる構文や文法が分かるので、英語力アップに役立ちます。

Index

はじめに ———— 002

Sandwich method 01
レストラン：電話で予約する
At a restaurant -
Making a reservation over the phone ———— 018

Sandwich method 02
レストラン：オーダーする
At a restaurant - Ordering food ———— 023

Sandwich method 03
ハンバーガーショップ：オーダーする
At a hamburger shop - Ordering food ———— 028

Sandwich method 04
マーケット：お土産を買う
At the market -
Buying souvenirs ———— 033

Sandwich method 05
美術館：音声ガイドを聞く
At the art museum -
Learning from the audio guide ———— 038

Sandwich method 06
劇場：ミュージカルを見る
At a theater - Seeing a musical ———— 043

Sandwich method 07
薬局：薬の説明を聞く
At a pharmacy -
Listening to information about the medicine ———— 048

Sandwich method 08	学校：説明を受ける At school - Receiving information about the school	053
Sandwich method 09	道案内：公共機関を利用して Getting directions - Using public transportation	058
Sandwich method 10	道案内：行き方を教わる Getting directions - Being told the way to go	063
Sandwich method 11	駅：切符の買い方を教わる At the station - Learning how to buy a ticket	068
Sandwich method 12	電車：車内アナウンスを聞く On the train - Listening to the train announcements	073
Sandwich method 13	飛行機：機内アナウンスを聞く On the airplane - Listening to the inflight announcements	078
Sandwich method 14	空港：到着ロビーでアナウンスを聞く In the arrival lobby - Listening to announcements	083
Sandwich method 15	タクシー：運転手と雑談する In the taxi - Chatting with the driver	088

Index

Sandwich method 16
ホテル：チェックインする
At the hotel - Checking in — 093

Sandwich method 17
ホテル：アクティビティについて聞く
At the hotel -
Receiving information about available activities — 098

Sandwich method 18
ホームステイ：家族のルールを教わる
During a homestay -
Learning the house rules — 103

Sandwich method 19
ホテル：換金方法について教わる
At the hotel -
Learning how to exchange money — 108

Sandwich method 20
テレビ：天気予報を見る
On TV - Watching the weather report — 113

Sandwich method 21
テレビ：スポーツニュースを見る
On TV - Watching the sports news — 118

Sandwich method 22
テレビ：料理番組を見る
On TV - Watching a cooking show — 123

Sandwich method 23
テレビ：通販番組を見る
On TV - Watching an infomercial — 128

さあ、さっそく
英語サンドイッチメソッドを
はじめましょう!

English Sandwich Method

Sandwich method 01

レストラン：電話で予約する

At a restaurant - Making a reservation over the phone

英文 英語の文章の全体像を確認しよう

Let me confirm: You'd like to make a reservation for five people for August 18 from 7:30 to 9:30. Is that right?

Okay, please wait for just a moment, and I'll check and see if we have an opening.

Thank you for waiting, I'm afraid that we're completely full, during those times, but if you could come a little earlier and leave at 9:00, then we can reserve a table for you. Actually, if you could arrive at around 6:30, then you probably don't even need to make reservations. We usually only get really busy at a little after 9:00 because that's when the opera ends.

Oh, just one moment. I have just been told that someone has canceled their reservation, so if you'd like, I can reserve a table for you from 8:00 to 10:00.

Okay, so I'll reserve a table for 8:00 for five people. I need to tell you that if you don't arrive by 10 minutes after 8:00 at the latest, then we may need to sit someone else at your table and you'll have to stand in line. Also, please call us if there are any changes in your plans. That would be really helpful.

サンドイッチ文 意味のまとまりで区切って考えよう

▶ <u>Let me confirm:</u>[*1]
確認させて

▶ You'd like to make a reservation for five people
あなたは5名の予約をしたい

for August 18 from 7:30 to 9:30.
8月18日の7時30分から9時30分まで

▶ Is that right?
それで合ってる？

▶ Okay, please wait for just a moment,
はい、ちょっと待ってください

and I'll check and see
調べてみます

if we have an opening.
空いているかどうか

▶ Thank you for waiting,
お待ちどうさま

I'm afraid that we're completely full,
あいにく満席のようです

during those times,
その時間は

but if you could come a little earlier
でも、もし少し前に来られるなら

and leave at 9:00,
そして、9時に帰る（なら）

then we can reserve a table for you.
そうであれば、あなたのためにテーブルを予約できる

▶ Actually,
実は

if you could arrive at around 6:30,
もし、あなたが6時30分頃に着けば

then you probably don't even need
それなら、たぶん必要もない

to make reservations.
予約をする

▶ We usually only get really busy
店はいつも（その時間）すごく混むだけ

at a little after 9:00
9時少し過ぎが

because that's when the opera ends.
オペラが終わるから

▶ Oh, just one moment.
おお、ちょっと待って

▶ I have just been told that*2
今、連絡が入った

someone has canceled their reservation,
予約のキャンセルが出たと

so if you'd like,
だから、よければ

I can reserve a table for you from 8:00 to 10:00.
8時から10時にテーブルを予約できる

▶ Okay, so I'll reserve a table
はい、では予約を入れよう

for 8:00 for five people.
8時に5名で

▶ I need to tell you
伝えておく

that if you don't arrive by 10 minutes after 8:00 at the latest,
8時を10分過ぎても来なければ

then we may need to sit someone else at your table
ほかのだれかに席を譲らなければならないかもしれない

and you'll have to stand in line.
そしてあなたは列に並ばなければならない

▶ Also, please call us
それと、電話してください

if there are any changes in your plans.
何か変更があったら

▶ That would be really helpful.[3]
（電話をくれると）とても助かる。

Keywords キーワード

confirm	確認する
make a reservation	予約する
see if...	～かどうか確かめる
opening	空き、すき間

be afraid that...	(残念ながら)～だと思う
even	～さえも、～すらも
at the latest	遅くとも
stand in line	列に並ぶ

Points ポイント

*1（P.19）
Let me confirm:
「確認させて」という主旨を伝えコロンで区切るのは、説明が長くなるときにネイティブがよく使う方法。確認してもらいたいことは、「その内容は……」と後に続けます。

*2（P.20）
I have just been told that...
「今、～と聞かされたところです」という表現。能動態では（特定できる誰か）told me that...となり、主語にあたる「誰か」がないと英文にならないので、「誰が」よりも「何が」を伝えたいときは受動態で表現します。

*3（P.21）
That would be really helpful.
That would be really helpful if you could call us.からif節を省略した一文。仮定法のなごりでwouldが残っています。「電話をしていただけると仮定した場合」と一歩引いた控えめな印象。

日本語訳　文章全体としての訳し方を確認しよう

　以下の内容でよいか確認させてください。ご予約は、8月18日の7時30分から9時30分に5名様ですね？
　かしこまりました。少々お待ちください。空いているかどうかをお調べします。
　お待たせいたしました。そのお時間は満席なのですが、もし少し前にいらして9時にお帰りになるのであれば、テーブルをご用意いたします。実は、6時30分頃ご到着されれば、おそらくご予約すら必要ございません。オペラが終わる9時を少し過ぎた頃だけが、本当にひどく混むだけなのです。
　あ、少々お待ちください。ただ今、予約のキャンセルが出たと連絡が入りましたので、よろしければ8時から10時までテーブルをお取りできます。
　はい、では、8時に5名様で予約を入れておきます。もし8時を10分過ぎても到着されない場合は、ほかの方に席をお譲りしますので、順番を待っていただかないとなりません。何か変更される場合は、お電話をいただけると助かります。

Sandwich method 02

レストラン：オーダーする
At a restaurant - Ordering food

英文 英語の文章の全体像を確認しよう

Good evening. Do you have a reservation?

Oh, I see. Well, I'm afraid we don't have any free tables right now. If you could wait for a few minutes, I think a table will become available soon. There are two in your party, right? Oh, it looks like there is a free table now, and it's by the window. Is that okay with you?

Okay, here are your menus. Our special tonight is the New York steak. You can order it a la carte or you can get the set. The set comes with a green salad, the soup of the day and a baked potato with butter and sour cream.

Oh, you're vegetarian? We have some really nice salads. I recommend the Chef's Salad. I can replace the meat with extra tomatoes, if you'd like. And all the salads come with all-you-can-eat French bread.

Would you like some coffee, tea or something else to drink while you decide?

Okay, sure. Please take your time and let me know when you're ready to order.

サンドイッチ文 意味のまとまりで区切って考えよう

▶ **Good evening.**
いらっしゃいませ

Do you have a reservation?
予約はある？

▶ **Oh, I see.**
ああ、はい

▶ **Well, I'm afraid**
うーん。申し訳ないけれど

we don't have any free tables right now.
今空いているテーブルはないと思う

▶ **If you could wait for a few minutes,**
もし、あなたが2、3分待てるなら

I think a table will become available soon.
テーブルはすぐに空くと思う

▶ **There are two in your party, right?**
二人であってる？

▶ **Oh, it looks like there is a free table now,**
ああ、今、一つテーブルがあるようだ

and it's by the window.
そしてそれは窓際だ

▶ <u>**Is that okay with you?**</u>[1]
それでいい？

▶ **Okay, here are your menus.**
では、メニューをどうぞ

- Our special tonight is[*2] the New York steak.
  今夜のスペシャルは、ニューヨーク・ステーキ
- You can order it a la carte or you can get the set.
  アラカルトでもセットでもオーダーができる
- The set comes with a green salad,
  セットメニューにはグリーン・サラダがついてくる

  the soup of the day and a baked potato with butter and sour cream.
  日替わりスープ、ベイクド・ポテトのバターとサワークリーム添えも（ついてくる）
- Oh, you're vegetarian?
  あ、あなたはベジタリアン？
- We have some really nice salads.
  すごくおいしいサラダがある
- I recommend the Chef's Salad.
  シェフ・サラダをおすすめする
- I can replace the meat with extra tomatoes,
  肉のかわりにトマトの追加ができる

  if you'd like.
  もしよければ
- And all the salads come with
  それにすべてのサラダについている

  all-you-can-eat French bread.
  フランスパンの食べ放題が

▶ **Would you like some coffee, tea or something else**
コーヒーかお茶などはどう？
to drink while you decide?
（注文を）決める間に飲む

▶ **Okay, sure.**
ええ、もちろん

▶ **Please take your time**[*3]
どうぞごゆっくり
and let me know
私に声をかけて
when you're ready to order.
注文が決まったら

Keywords キーワード

in your party あなたの一行、グループ

come with... 〜がついている

replace A with B AをBに交換する

all-you-can-eat 食べ放題の

Points ポイント

*1（P.24）
Is that okay with you?

「よろしいですか？」と確認するときによく使われる表現。Is that okay? とも言いますが、with youを付けると相手を尊重した丁寧な印象に。for youとは言わないので間違えないように。

*2（P.25）
Our special tonight is...

「おすすめは〜」は、Tonight's special is...（今夜のおすすめは〜）とも言われます。

*3（P.26）
Please take your time...

「あなたの時間をかけて」という意味から、「急がなくていいからね」「ごゆっくり」というニュアンスに。待ち合わせに遅れている人に「ゆっくり来てね」と言うときにも使えます。

日本語訳 文章全体としての訳し方を確認しよう

いらっしゃいませ。ご予約はされていますか？

ああはい、わかりました。うーん、そうですね。あいにく、ただ今、ご案内できるお席（テーブル）はございません。でも、2、3分お待ちいただけるようでしたら、（お席を）ご用意できます。お二人様でよろしいでしょうか？　あ、ただ今窓際のテーブルが準備できました。そちらでよろしいでしょうか？

では、メニューをどうぞ。今夜のスペシャルは、ニューヨーク・ステーキです。アラカルトでもセットでもご注文いただけます。セットには、グリーン・サラダ、日替わりスープ、ベイクド・ポテトのバターとサワークリーム添えがついております。

あ、ベジタリアンでいらっしゃいますか？（では、）たいへんおいしいサラダをご用意しております。シェフ・サラダがおすすめです。お肉のかわりにトマトの追加ができますが、いかがでしょうか。そして、すべてのサラダにフランスパンの食べ放題がついております。

ご注文が決まるまでの間に、コーヒーかお茶はいかがですか？

ええ、もちろん（お持ちいたします）。ご注文の際はお声がけください、それまで、どうぞごゆっくり。

Sandwich method 03

 # ハンバーガーショップ：オーダーする

At a hamburger shop - Ordering food

英文 英語の文章の全体像を確認しよう

Good afternoon and welcome to Hank's Burgers! Are you ready to place your order? Is this for here or to go?

Okay, one veggie burger with avocado. Would you like a side order with that? In addition to French fries we also have onion rings, green salad, potato salad, soup, and mashed potatoes with gravy. Our soup of the day is minestrone.

Okay, one green salad. What kind of dressing would you like on that? Our choices are French, Italian, and ranch dressing.

Okay, Italian dressing. Can I get you a drink with that?

Okay, one medium iced tea.

So, that's one veggie burger with avocado, one green salad with Italian dressing, and one medium iced tea. I can give you the combo meal price. Not only do you save $1.80 over the a la carte menu price, right now we're offering a free sample of our new soft-serve ice cream with all combo meals. Can I get you anything else? All right, your total is $9.30. Enjoy your meal!

サンドイッチ文 意味のまとまりで区切って考えよう

▶ Good afternoon and welcome to Hank's Burgers!
こんにちは、ハンクのハンバーガーへようこそ！

▶ <u>Are</u> <u>you ready</u> <u>to place</u> <u>your order?</u>[*1]
注文は決まった？

▶ Is this for here or to go?
店内それともお持ち帰り？

▶ Okay, one veggie burger with avocado.
では、アボカド付きの野菜バーガーを一つ

▶ Would you like a side order with that?
サイドオーダーはいかが？

▶ In addition to French fries
フライドポテトのほかに

we also have onion rings, green salad, potato salad, soup,
私たち（の店）には、オニオンリング、グリーンサラダ、ポテトサラダ、スープもある

and mashed potatoes with gravy.
それにグレイビーソース添えのマッシュポテトも（ある）

▶ Our soup of the day is minestrone.
本日のスープはミネストローネ

▶ Okay, one green salad.
オーケー、グリーンサラダ一つ

▶ What kind of dressing would you like on that?
ドレッシングは何がいい？

▶ Our choices are French, Italian, and ranch dressing.
フレンチ、イタリアン、ランチドレッシングがある

▶ Okay, Italian dressing.
ではイタリアンドレッシングで

▶ Can I get you a drink with that?
ドリンクをつける？

▶ Okay, one medium iced tea.
オーケー、アイスティーのミディアムを一つ

▶ So, that's one veggie burger with avocado,
では、野菜バーガー・アボカド添えを一つ

one green salad with Italian dressing,
イタリアンドレッシングのグリーンサラダを一つ

and one medium iced tea.
それと、ミディアムのアイスティー一つ

▶ I can give you the combo meal price.[*2]
あなたに、コンボ料金を提供できる

▶ Not only do you save $1.80[*3]
1ドル80セント節約できるだけでなく

over the a la carte menu price,
アラカルト料金よりも

right now we're offering
今、私たちが提供している

a free sample of our new soft-serve ice cream
試食用のソフトクリームを

with all combo meals.
すべてのコンボメニューと一緒に

▶ Can I get you anything else?
ほかに何か？

▶ All right, your total is $9.30.
では、合計で９ドル30セント

▶ Enjoy your meal!
ごゆっくり！

Keywords キーワード

for here or to go
店内（で食べる）か、お持ち帰りか

veggie 野菜
＊vegetableのカジュアルな言い方

in addition to... 〜に加えて

soft-serve ice cream
ソフトクリーム

Enjoy your meal.
ごゆっくり食事を楽しんで

Points ポイント

*1 (P.29)
Are you ready to place your order?

place (your) orderで「注文する、発注する」の意味。あらたまった表現なので軽いニュアンスでは、Are you ready to make your order?やAre you ready to order?とも。

*2 (P.30)
I can give you the combo meal price.

日本語だと「当店」のように主語が自分個人ではないので「We」を使いたくなりますが、英語のニュアンスでは、サービスの権限が担当者に委ねられているため主語は「I」になります。

*3 (P.30)
Not only do you save $1.80...

本来はYou don't only save $1.80...ですが、「強調のための倒置」を使って文頭にNot onlyを移動させた表現。Not onlyの後は疑問形なので、doとyouの語順も入れ替えになります。

日本語訳　文章全体としての訳し方を確認しよう

　こんにちは。ハンクのハンバーガーへようこそ！　ご注文はお決まりですか？　店内でお召し上がりですか？　それともお持ち帰りですか？
　かしこまりました、野菜バーガー・アボカド添えをお一つですね。サイドメニューはいかがですか？ フライドポテトのほかに、オニオンリング、グリーンサラダ、ポテトサラダ、スープ、それにグレイビーソース添えのマッシュポテトがございます。本日のスープはミネストローネです。
　かしこまりました、グリーンサラダをお一つですね。ドレッシングはどちらにしましょうか？ フレンチ、イタリアン、ランチドレッシングから選べます。
　かしこまりました、イタリアンドレッシングですね。ドリンクはいかがですか？
　かしこまりました、アイスティーのミディアムをお一つですね。
　では、野菜バーガー・アボカド添えをお一つ、イタリアンドレッシングのグリーンサラダをお一つ、ミディアム（サイズ）のアイスティーをお一つで、ご注文をお受けしました。アラカルトでご注文されるより、1ドル80セントお得なコンボプライスで提供できますし、今ならどのコンボメニューにも試食用のソフトクリームがついてきますよ。ほかのご注文はありませんか？
　はい。合計で9ドル30セントです。どうぞごゆっくり！

Sandwich method 04

マーケット：お土産を買う

At the market - Buying souvenirs

英文　英語の文章の全体像を確認しよう

　Hello, there! Have you ever seen this? This is called dried fruit leather, and it's been a popular treat from this region for a very long time. It's kind of tough, but if you suck on it, it melts in your mouth. This dried fruit leather is made from locally grown fruit. It's unique and tastes delicious, so many people buy it as a gift.

　It'll stay fresh for about two weeks outside the refrigerator, but if you keep it cold, it'll stay fresh for at least four or five months, so you can buy quite a lot of it. Last week a customer from Japan bought 10 pounds of this! It was too heavy for him to carry, so we sent it by express delivery, and I heard that he received it in only three days. I'm sure your parents would be really happy if you sent them some dried fruit leather. It would give them a chance to enjoy the local flavors here.

　If you buy a lot, I'll give you a discount! If you buy five sheets, I'll give you 20 percent off. Would you like to try a bit?

サンドイッチ文　意味のまとまりで区切って考えよう

▶ Hello, there!
やあ、こんにちは！

▶ Have you ever seen this?
これ、見たことある？

▶ This is called dried fruit leather,
これはドライフルーツ・レザーって呼ばれていて

and it's been a popular treat from this region
この地域ではポピュラーなスイーツだ

for a very long time.
かなり前から

▶ It's kind of tough,
それは少し固い

but if you suck on it,
でも、しゃぶっていると

it melts in your mouth.
口の中でとける

▶ This dried fruit leather is made
このドライフルーツ・レザーはできている

from locally grown fruit.[*1]
この土地で育った果物で

▶ It's unique and tastes delicious,
独特で味もおいしい

so many people buy it as a gift.
だから、お土産物にする人が多い

▶ It'll stay fresh for about two weeks
これはだいたい2週間もつ
outside the refrigerator,
冷蔵庫に入れなくても
but if you keep it cold,
でも、冷蔵すると
it'll stay fresh for at least four or five months,
最低でも4、5か月は新鮮なままだ
so you can buy quite a lot of it.
なので、大量に買っても大丈夫

▶ Last week a customer from Japan
先週日本から来た客が
bought 10 pounds of this!
10ポンド（約4.5kg）もこれを買った
It was too heavy for him to carry,
持って帰るのが彼には重すぎた
so we sent it by express delivery,
だから、うちから速達で送った
and I heard that he received it in only three days.
そうしたら、日本に3日で着いたらしい

▶ I'm sure your parents would be really happy
あなたの両親はすごく喜ぶと思う
if you sent them*2 some dried fruit leather.
もしドライフルーツ・レザーを送ってあげたら

▸ **It would give them a chance**
彼らにチャンスをあげられる
to enjoy the local flavors here.
ここの味を楽しむ

If you buy a lot,
もし、たくさん買ってくれるなら
I'll give you a discount!
値引きしよう

▸ **If you buy five sheets,**
もし5枚買ったら
I'll give you 20 percent off.[*3]
2割引にしてあげる

▸ **Would you like to try a bit?**
ひとつ味見してみない?

Keywords キーワード

Hello, there!	皆さん、こんにちは!
treat	おやつ、スイーツ
region	地域、一帯
suck on	〜をしゃぶる
unique	変わった、唯一の
stay	〜のままでいる
bit	少し、ちょっと

Points ポイント

*1（P.34）
This dried fruit leather is made from locally grown fruit.

「〜でできている」はmade from...（一見して原料がわからないもの）とmade of...（目で見て材料がわかるもの）で使い分けます。そのため、ドライフルーツ・レザーはfrom。

*2（P.35）
I'm sure your parents would be really happy if you sent them...

〈I'm sure A if B.〉で、「BであればAだと私は確信している」という構文。「you sent them...であれば、your parents would be really happyだと確信する」という意味。

*3（P.36）
...I'll give you 20 percent off.

20%オフには XX percent discountという言い方もありますが、その場合は必ず冠詞が必要です。I'll give you a 20 percent discount.（2割引きしますよ）となります。

日本語訳　文章全体としての訳し方を確認しよう

　こんにちは！　これ、見たことある？　これはドライフルーツ・レザーと言って、このへんでは昔からポピュラーなスイーツなんです。ちょっと固いけど、しゃぶっていると口の中でとろけますよ！　このドライフルーツ・レザーは、すべて地元産の果物を使っていて、独特で味もおいしいから、お土産物にする人も多いんです。

　これは冷蔵庫に入れなくても2週間くらいもちますが、冷蔵すると最低でも4、5か月保存可能なので、たくさん買っても大丈夫です。先週、これを10ポンド（約4.5kg）も買った日本のお客様がいたんですよ！　持って帰るには重すぎたから、商品をうちから速達で送ったんですけど、日本までたった3日で届いたそうですよ。ご両親にドライフルーツ・レザーを送ってあげたら喜ぶと思います。ご両親にこちらの味を楽しんでいただけますよ。

　まとめて買っていただけたら、おまけしますよ！　5枚買っていただけたら2割引にします。ひとつ試食してみませんか？

Sandwich method 05

美術館：音声ガイドを聞く

At the art museum - Learning from the audio guide

英文 英語の文章の全体像を確認しよう

　This large painting is called "The Birth of Venus," and it's well-known as Sandro Botticelli's masterpiece. Painted on canvas with tempera paint, it's 173 centimeters high and 279 centimeters wide. Just like his other famous piece, "Primavera," its subject matter is based around Greek mythology.

　A new-born Venus, the goddess of love and beauty, moves with the waves riding a shell. Horae, the goddess of the seasons, is dancing gracefully for Venus to the right with her red cloak opened and ready to embrace her.

　We can sense the wind, the freshness of Spring and the elegance of Venus coming right from the painting. The wind that moves along the painting from left to right causes Venus's hair to flutter and gracefully fans Horae's cloak. With the happiness of the Mediterranean Sea in Spring overflowing in the painting, it's wonderfully fitting for the birth of Venus.

　Sandro Botticelli is a painter of the Florentine school of the Early Renaissance, and he spent the most of his life in Florence. Unlike previous painters, he used clear outlines and thin, delicate lines rather than accurate perspective.

サンドイッチ文　意味のまとまりで区切って考えよう

▶ **This large painting is called "The Birth of Venus,"**
この大作は『ヴィーナスの誕生』と呼ばれていて、

and it's well-known as Sandro Botticelli's masterpiece.
サンドロ・ボッティチェリの代表作としてよく知られている

▶ <u>Painted on canvas with tempera paint,</u>[*1]
カンバスにテンペラで描かれている

it's 173 centimeters high and 279 centimeters wide.
縦173cm、幅279cmある

▶ **Just like his other famous piece, "Primavera,"**
もう一つの彼の有名な代表作『春（ラ・プリマヴェーラ）』と同様に

its subject matter is based around Greek mythology.
ギリシャ神話をもとにしたテーマ

▶ **A new-born Venus,**
生まれたばかりのヴィーナス

the goddess of love and beauty,
（それは）美と愛の女神

moves with the waves riding a shell.
貝殻に乗って波の上を移動している

▶ **Horae, the goddess of the seasons,**
季節の女神ホーラが

is dancing gracefully for Venus to the right
右側では、ヴィーナスのために軽快に舞っている

with her red cloak opened and ready to embrace her.
赤いマントを広げて彼女（ヴィーナス）を包み込む準備をして

▶ We can sense the wind,
感じることができる。風と

the freshness of Spring
春の季節のみずみずしさと

and the elegance of Venus
ヴィーナスの輝きを

coming right from the painting.*2
この作品からじかに伝わってくる

▶ The wind that moves along the painting
絵の中を流れる風は

from left to right
左から右に

causes Venus's hair to flutter
ヴィーナスの髪をなびかせ

and gracefully fans Horae's cloak.
ホーラの持つマントを優雅にあおる

▶ With the happiness of the Mediterranean Sea in Spring
春の地中海の幸福感が

overflowing in the painting,
画面にあふれていて

it's wonderfully fitting
とてもテーマに合っている

for the birth of Venus.*3
ヴィーナスの誕生という

▶ Sandro Botticelli is a painter
サンドロ・ボッティチェリは画家

of the Florentine school of the Early Renaissance,
初期ルネサンスのフィレンツェ派の

and he spent the most of his life in Florence.
そして、生涯ほとんどフィレンツェで過ごした

▶ Unlike previous painters,
それまでの画家の手法とは違い

he used clear outlines
明確な輪郭や

and thin, delicate lines
繊細な描線を用いた

rather than accurate perspective.
正確な遠近法ではなく

Keywords キーワード

masterpiece	最高傑作、代表作
tempera	テンペラ(西洋絵画の手法)
subject matter	題材
Greek mythology	ギリシャ神話
gracefully	優美に、滑らかに
cloak	マント
embrace	包みこむ
flutter	はためく
school	(芸術・学問などの)一派、一門
previous	以前の
accurate	正確な
perspective	遠近法

Points ポイント

*1（P.39）
Painted on canvas with tempera paint,
文頭の〈主語＋be動詞〉(It's) が省略されています。

*2（P.40）
…coming right from the painting.
coming from the paintingで「絵から来る」。ここにrightを加えると「真っ直ぐに」「まさしく」という意味が加味され、この絵画が伝えるインパクトを強調できます。

*3（P.40）
…it's wonderfully fitting for the birth of Venus.
fit for...は「〜に適している」「〜にふさわしい」という意味。fit to...（〜に適している）は、サイズや構造など、より物理的な意味で適したときに使われるので、芸術鑑賞にはforを。

日本語訳 文章全体としての訳し方を確認しよう

　この大作は、サンドロ・ボッティチェリの代表作としてよく知られている『ヴィーナスの誕生』です。カンバスにテンペラで描かれ、縦173cm、幅279cmあります。もう一つの、彼の有名な代表作『春（ラ・プリマヴェーラ）』と同様に、ギリシャ神話をテーマにした作品です。
　生まれたばかりの、美と愛の女神ヴィーナスが、貝殻に乗って波の上を移動しています。右側では、季節の女神ホーラが、軽快に舞いながら、ヴィーナスを赤いマントで包もうとしています。
　この作品から、ヴィーナスの輝き、春の季節のみずみずしさが伝わってきます。左から右に流れる風は、ヴィーナスの髪をなびかせ、ホーラの持つマントを優雅にあおります。春の地中海の幸福感が画面にあふれていて、ヴィーナスの誕生というテーマにふさわしい作品です。
　サンドロ・ボッティチェリは、初期ルネサンスのフィレンツェ派の画家で、生涯のほとんどをフィレンツェで過ごしました。それまでの画家の手法とは違い、正確な遠近法は使わず、明確な輪郭や繊細な描線が特徴的です。

Sandwich method 06

劇場：ミュージカルを見る
At a theater - Seeing a musical

英文 英語の文章の全体像を確認しよう

Today's scheduled performance is "Les Miserables." The long-running hit will soon be celebrating its 30th anniversary.

It's based on the novel by Victor Hugo and set during the 19th century French Revolution. It's the story of a man who was imprisoned for 19 years for stealing a loaf of bread. It follows his life from his return to the outside world until his death and deals with themes such as poverty, love, revolution and dignity.

In this new production, the rotating stage used in previous performances has been eliminated, and the stage backdrop shows paintings by the author. Please enjoy the beautiful voice of Ramin Karimloo starring as Jean Valjean.

Performances are twice daily, at 2:00 and 8:00. Seating options are orchestra, front mezzanine, and rear mezzanine. The further from the stage, the lower the seat prices are. There will be only one performance tomorrow, starting at 7:00. Doors open 30 minutes before curtain, and there's a 15 minute intermission. Food and drink are strictly prohibited except for in the lobby. Thank you for your cooperation.

サンドイッチ文 意味のまとまりで区切って考えよう

▶ Today's scheduled performance is "Les Miserables."
本日公演が予定されているのは『レ・ミゼラブル』

▶ The long-running hit
このロングランヒット作品は

will soon be celebrating its 30th anniversary.
もうすぐ30周年を迎える

▶ It's based on the novel by Victor Hugo
本作品は、ヴィクトル・ユーゴーの小説に基づいている

and set during the 19th century French Revolution.
そして、19世紀のフランス革命が舞台である

▶ It's the story of a man
ある男の話である

who was imprisoned for 19 years
19年間投獄された

for stealing a loaf of bread.
パンを盗んだことで

▶ It follows his life
この作品は、彼の人生を追っている

from his return to the outside world until his death
彼が外の世界へ戻ってから、死ぬまでの

and deals with themes
また、(この後説明するような) テーマを扱っている

such as poverty, love, revolution and dignity.[1]
「貧困」「愛」「革命」「尊厳」など

▶ **In this new production,**
この新演出では

the rotating stage used in previous performances
前作まで使われていた回転式舞台は

has been eliminated,
なくなった

and the stage backdrop shows
さらに、舞台背景に見せている

paintings by the author.
原作者の絵を

▶ **Please enjoy the beautiful voice of Ramin Karimloo**
ラミン・カリムルーの歌声をお楽しみください

starring as Jean Valjean.
ジャン・バルジャン役を演じる

▶ **Performances are twice daily,**
公演は、1日2回で

at 2:00 and 8:00.
2時からと8時からである

▶ **Seating options are orchestra, front mezzanine, and rear mezzanine.**
座席のタイプは「オーケストラ」と「2階前方」、「2階後方」がある

▶ <u>**The further from the stage,**</u>
ステージから遠ければ遠いほど

the lower the seat prices are.*2
チケットの値段は安くなる

▶ There will be only one performance tomorrow,
明日の公演は1回限りである

starting at 7:00.
7時開始（である）

▶ Doors open 30 minutes before curtain,
開演30分前から開場する

and there's a 15 minute intermission.
また、15分の休憩がある

▶ Food and drink are strictly prohibited
飲食は固く禁じられている

except for in the lobby.
ロビーを除いて

▶ Thank you for your cooperation.*3
ご協力ありがとうございます

Keywords キーワード

imprison 投獄する	**stage backdrop** 舞台背景（の幕）
poverty 貧困	**mezzanine** 2階席
dignity 尊厳	**rear** 後部の
rotating stage 回転式舞台	**curtain** （劇場の）開演
eliminate 取り除く	**intermission** 休憩、幕あい

Points ポイント

＊1（P.44）
...deals with themes such as poverty, love, revolution and dignity.
deal with...は「取り組む」などの意味で日常的に使われる表現ですが、ここでは「（テーマとして）取り上げる」という意味。テーマの説明はsuch as（たとえば）の後に続きます。

＊2（P.45）
The further from the stage, the lower the seat prices are.
〈the＋比較級, the＋比較級〉は「～であればあるほど、さらに～」という意味。the further「遠ければ遠いほど」the lower「低くなる」となります。

＊3（P.46）
Thank you for your cooperation.
「ご協力ありがとうございます」という決まり文句。公共の場でよく耳にします。

日本語訳 文章全体としての訳し方を確認しよう

　本日公演が予定されているのは（ミュージカルの）『レ・ミゼラブル』です。もうすぐ30周年となるロングランヒット作品です。
　本作品は、ヴィクトル・ユーゴーが19世紀のフランス革命を舞台に描いた小説が原作です。パンを盗んだことで19年も投獄されていた男の話です。外の世界へ戻るところから、生涯を終えるまでを描いた物語で、「貧困」「愛」「革命」「尊厳」がテーマの作品です。
　新演出では、これまで使われていた回転式舞台をなくし、舞台背景には原作者の絵を取り入れています。ジャン・バルジャン役を演じるラミン・カリムルーの歌声をお楽しみください。
　2時からと8時からの2回公演で、座席はオーケストラ、2階前方、2階後方がございます。ステージから遠くなるほど、チケットの価格は下がります。明日の公演は1回で、7時からです。開演30分前から開場し、途中で15分の休憩をはさみます。ロビー以外での飲食は固くお断りしております。ご協力をお願いいたします。

Sandwich method **07**

薬局：薬の説明を聞く
At a pharmacy - Listening to information about the medicine

英文 英語の文章の全体像を確認しよう

　If you have a fever, then I recommend this new medicine. We just started selling it a few weeks ago. It's a little more expensive than other cold medicines here, but it's really popular. You'll need to take two capsules after every meal, and there's enough medicine for 10 days.

　If your fever isn't too high, then this medicine here should be fine. It will help with a sore throat and other cold symptoms. However, both of these medicines will make you drowsy, so you had better not take any medicine until you get back to your hotel.

　When traveling, it's sometimes hard to get enough sleep. Maybe that's why you got sick. If you take the medicine for a few days and get lots of rest, I think you'll feel better soon.

　You've had your cold for two weeks? That's a long time for a cold, so you should see a doctor about this. There's a clinic just across the street. They're open until 8:00 this evening, so if you'd like I can call and make an appointment for you.

サンドイッチ文 意味のまとまりで区切って考えよう

- If you have a fever,

  熱があるなら

  then I recommend this new medicine.

  この新しい薬をおすすめする

- We just started selling it a few weeks ago.

  2、3週間前から発売し始めたばかり

- It's a little more expensive than other cold medicines here,

  ここにあるほかの風邪薬より少し高い

  but it's really popular.

  でもとても評判がいい

- You'll need to take two capsules

  2カプセル飲む必要がある

  after every meal,

  毎食後に

  and there's enough medicine for 10 days.

  そして10日分の薬がある

- If your fever isn't too high,

  もし、それほど高熱でなければ

  then this medicine here should be fine.[1]

  この薬でいいでしょう

- It will help with a sore throat

  これは、のどの痛みに効く

and other cold symptoms.
それと、ほかの風邪の症状にも

▶ However,
ただ

both of these medicines will make you drowsy,
これらの薬は両方とも眠気を誘う

so you had better not take any medicine
なので、どの薬も服用しないほうがいい

until you get back to your hotel.
ホテルに戻るまでは

▶ When traveling,
旅行中は

it's sometimes hard to get enough sleep.*2
充分に眠れないこともある

▶ Maybe that's why you got sick.
たぶんそれが具合が悪くなる原因だ

▶ If you take the medicine for a few days
もし、数日間この薬を飲めば

and get lots of rest,
そして休養すれば

I think you'll feel better soon.
すぐに回復すると思う

▶ You've had your cold for two weeks?*3
2週間も風邪をひいているの？

- **That's a long time for a cold,**
  風邪にしては長い
  so you should see a doctor about this.
  なので、医者に診てもらうといい
- **There's a clinic just across the street.**
  ちょうど通りの向こう側にクリニックがある
- **They're open until 8:00 this evening,**
  夜8時まで開いている
  so if you'd like
  もしよければ
  I can call and make an appointment for you.
  私が電話であなたの予約を取ってあげる

Keywords キーワード

fever	熱	**symptom**	症状
capsule	カプセル、錠	**drowsy**	眠い
sore throat	のどの痛み	**rest**	休養、休息
		appointment	予約

Points ポイント

*1（P.49）
...this medicine here should be fine.
shouldは、推量ではあるものの強い希望と自信が含まれています。「私がおすすめするこの薬はきっと効きますよ」と、相手を安心させる言い回しです。

*2（P.50）
When traveling, it's sometimes hard to get enough sleep.
When travelingは、when you travelを端的に表したもの。このyouは「あなた」ではなく「人は誰でも」のニュアンスなので、「一般的に旅先では寝不足になる」という意味に。

*3（P.50）
You've had your cold for two weeks?
〈have＋had...〉という現在完了形を使った文。過去のある時点（2週間前）からずっと（継続して）風邪をひいていた」ことを表すので、haveが2つ重なっていても自然な表現です。

日本語訳　文章全体としての訳し方を確認しよう

　熱があるのでしたら、この薬がおすすめですよ。2、3週間前から発売し始めたばかりなんです。ここにあるほかの風邪薬より少しお高いですが、とても評判がいいんですよ。10日分ありますので、毎食後2錠（カプセル）ずつお飲みください。
　もしそれほど高熱ではないなら、こちらの薬でいいでしょう。のどの痛みとほかの風邪の症状に効きます。ただ、どちらも眠気を誘うので、ホテルに戻るまでは服用しないでください。
　旅行中は、充分眠れないこともあります。たぶんそれで具合が悪くなるんです。数日間この薬を飲んで休養すれば、すぐに治ると思いますよ。
　あなたは2週間も風邪をひいているんですか？　風邪にしては長いので、医者に診てもらったほうがいいかもしれません。ちょうど通りの向こう側にクリニックがあります。夜8時まで開いているので、よろしければ私が電話で予約をお取りしましょう。

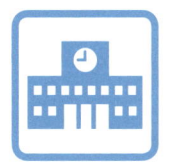

Sandwich method 08

学校：説明を受ける
At school - Receiving information about the school

英文 英語の文章の全体像を確認しよう

ABC Language School is a private language school established in 1980. It's one of the newer language schools in Los Angeles, but our friendly atmosphere has made us quite popular.

Using our unique materials and curriculum, we are committed to providing the best English education. We teach English required for daily life. And we also prepare students to study at a university level. In addition to general English courses, we offer academic preparation courses, business English courses, and intensive English courses. We cater our instruction to meet the needs of each and every student. Courses are offered throughout the year and each semester is 10 weeks; however, it is possible to extend the program length.

We also actively promote international exchange by hosting cultural events with the local community.

Class sizes are kept small, with approximately 10 students per class. Classes are divided into six levels. Students have the option of staying in the dormitories, or we can introduce homestay options.

Finally, we offer career counseling and advice to job-seekers.

サンドイッチ文 意味のまとまりで区切って考えよう

▶ ABC Language School
ABCランゲージ・スクールは

is a private language school established in 1980.
1980年に創立された私立の語学学校である

▶ It's one of the newer language schools in Los Angeles,
ロサンゼルスにある語学学校の中では新しい

but our friendly atmosphere
でも、フレンドリーな校風が

has made us quite popular.
なかなか人気となっている

▶ Using our unique materials and curriculum,
独自の教材とカリキュラムを使い

we are committed[*1]
私たちは努めている

to providing the best English education.
最高の英語教育を提供することに

▶ We teach English
私たちは英語を教えている

required for daily life.
日常生活に必要な

▶ And we also prepare students
さらに、学生に（語学の）準備もさせている

to study at a university level.
大学進学を前提とした

- ▶ In addition to general English courses,
  一般的な英語コースのほかに
  we offer academic preparation courses,
  進学準備コースがある
  business English courses, and intensive English courses.
  ビジネス英語コースと、集中英語コースもある
- ▶ We cater our instruction
  私たちは教育を提供している
  to meet the needs of each and every student.[2]
  すべての生徒のそれぞれのニーズに応じた
- ▶ Courses are offered throughout the year
  コースは一年を通して開講されている
  and each semester is 10 weeks;
  それぞれの期間は10週間
  however,
  でも
  it is possible to extend the program length.
  延長も可能である
- ▶ We also actively promote international exchange
  国際文化交流も積極的に進めている
  by hosting cultural events
  文化的イベントを主催することで

with the local community.
地域社会の人たちと

▶ Class sizes are kept small,
クラスの規模は少人数制を保ち

with approximately 10 students per class.
１クラス10名程度

▶ Classes are divided into six levels.*3
クラスはレベル別に６つに分かれている

▶ Students have the option of staying in the dormitories,
生徒の滞在施設として、寮がある

or we can introduce homestay options.
また、ホームステイ先の紹介もしている

▶ Finally, we offer career counseling
最後に、私たちは進路相談をしている

and advice to job-seekers.
そして就職活動のアドバイスも

Keywords キーワード

establish	設立する	intensive	集中的な
atmosphere	雰囲気	cater	応じる
be committed to...	～に専念する	offer	提供する
be required for...	～に必要な	approximately	およそ

Points ポイント

*1 (P.54)
Using our unique materials and curriculum, we are committed...

分詞構文のUsing（～を使いながら）は、主文we are committed...（私たちは～に努めている）を補足する一文。カンマで区切って意味を整理すると、聞き取りやすくなります。

*2 (P.55)
...to meet the needs of each and every student.

meet the needsで「ニーズに応じる」、of each and every studentで「学生一人ひとりの」の意味。宣伝文句によく使われる表現です。

*3 (P.56)
Classes are divided into six levels.

〈A＋be動詞＋divided into＋B〉で「AはBに分けられる」の意味。separateは「分けて離す」、divideは「分類する」「きっちり（等分に）分ける」とニュアンスが違うので使い分けて。

日本語訳　文章全体としての訳し方を確認しよう

　ABCランゲージ・スクールは、1980年に創立された私立の語学学校です。ロサンゼルスにある語学学校の中では新しいほうですが、フレンドリーな校風が評判となっております。
　（本校では）独自の教材とカリキュラムを使い、最高の英語教育を提供しております。日常的な英語力だけでなく、大学進学を前提とした語学準備にも対応しております。一般的な英語コースのほかに、進学準備コース、ビジネス英語コース、集中英語コースがあります。本校では、生徒それぞれのニーズに応じた（きめ細やかな）教育を行っております。コースは、一年を通して開講され、期間は10週間ですが、場合によっては延長も可能です。
　また、地域の方と文化的イベントを催すなど、国際文化交流にも積極的に取り組んでおります。
　クラスは少人数制で、1クラス10名程度。レベルは6つに分かれております。滞在施設として寮もありますが、ホームステイ先の斡旋もしております。
　最後に、進学希望者に対しては進路相談、就職のアドバイスなども行っております。

Sandwich method **09**

道案内：
公共交通機関を利用して

Getting directions –
Using public transportation

英文 英語の文章の全体像を確認しよう

　The easiest way to get to the Metropolitan Museum from here is to go by taxi, but it costs about 80 euros. I recommend using public transportation.
　First you need to go to Centrale Station. You can get on bus 45 at the bus station in front of the hotel. A bus leaves every 15 minutes, and it takes about 30 minutes to get there.
　At Centrale Station, you need to buy a 12 euro ticket for Ferrari Station. The train leaves from Platform 7, and it'll take you about 20 minutes to get there. At Ferrari Station, I recommend getting a free map at the information center.
　You can walk to the Metropolitan Museum in just five minutes or so. They open at 9:00 AM and close at 5:00 PM, but it usually gets really crowded in the afternoon, so I recommend going in the morning.
　My telephone number is on this card, so if you get lost or have any problems, just give me a call. Have a nice time.

サンドイッチ文 意味のまとまりで区切って考えよう

▶ **The easiest way**
いちばん簡単な方法

to get to the Metropolitan Museum from here
ここからメトロポリタン美術館に行く

is to go by taxi,
（それは）タクシーだ

but it costs about 80 euros.
でも、80ユーロくらいかかる

▶ **I recommend using public transportation.**
公共の交通機関をおすすめする

▶ <u>First</u>[*1] **you need to go to Centrale Station.**
まず、チェントラーレ駅に行く必要がある

▶ **You can get on bus 45**
45番のバスで行ける

at the bus station in front of the hotel.
ホテルの前のバス停から

▶ **A bus leaves every 15 minutes,**
バスは15分おきに出る

and it takes about 30 minutes
そして30分くらいかかる

to get there.
そこまで

▶ At Centrale Station,
チェントラーレ駅で

you need to buy a 12 euro ticket for Ferrari Station.
フェラーリ駅までの切符を12ユーロで購入して

▶ The train leaves from Platform 7,
列車は7番線から出発し

and it'll take you about 20 minutes to get there.*2
約20分で到着する

▶ At Ferrari Station,
フェラーリ駅では

I recommend getting a free map at the information center.
インフォメーションセンターで無料の地図をもらうとよい

▶ You can walk to the Metropolitan Museum
メトロポリタン美術館へは、歩いて行ける

in just five minutes or so.
5分しかかからない

▶ They open at 9:00 AM and close at 5:00 PM,
開館は午前9時、閉館は午後5時

but it usually gets really crowded in the afternoon,
でも、いつも午後がとても混む

so I recommend going in the morning.
なので、朝に行くのがいい

▶ **My telephone number is on this card,**
このカードに私の電話番号が書いてある

so if you get lost or have any problems,
だから、もし道に迷ったり何かトラブルにあったら

just give me a call.
とにかく電話して

▶ <u>**Have a nice time.**</u>*3
行ってらっしゃい

Keywords キーワード

cost	費用がかかる
public transportation	公共の
bus station	バス乗り場、バス停
a 12 euro ticket	12ユーロ券
or so	くらいで、かそこらで
get crowded	混雑する
give a call	電話をかける

Points ポイント

*1 (P.59)
First...

順を追って説明するときに使われる、「まずは」という表現。At firstと、atを付けると微妙にニュアンスが変わり「最初は〜だったけど〜になった」という意味になるので注意。

*2 (P.60)
...it'll take you about 20 minutes to get there.

時間がどのくらいかかるかを教えるときは〈it'll take / it takes you＋時間＋to動詞〉を使います。It'll take about 20 minutes (for you) to get there.と言い換えることもできます。

*3 (P.61)
Have a nice time.

直訳すると「いい時間を」ですが、日本語の「行ってらっしゃい」のニュアンスで人を送り出すときにも使える表現。niceはgoodにも言い換えられます。

日本語訳 文章全体としての訳し方を確認しよう

　ここからメトロポリタン美術館へ行くのに、いちばん簡単な方法はタクシーですが、80ユーロくらいかかってしまいます。(だから)私は公共の交通機関をおすすめします。
　まず、チェントラーレ駅に行ってください。ホテル前のバス停から45番のバスに乗れば行けます。バスは15分おきに走っていて、そこへは30分くらいかかります。
　チェントラーレ駅で、フェラーリ駅までの切符を12ユーロで購入します。列車は7番線から出発し、(フェラーリ駅には)約20分で到着します。フェラーリ駅に着いたら、インフォメーションセンターで無料の地図をもらってください。
　メトロポリタン美術館へは、歩いて5分しかかかりません。開館は午前9時、閉館は午後5時ですが、いつも午後がとても混むので朝に行くのがいいでしょう。
　このカードに私の電話番号が書いてありますので、道に迷ったり何かトラブルがあったら、とにかく電話してください。では行ってらっしゃい。

Sandwich method 10

道案内：行き方を教わる
**Getting directions -
Being told the way to go**

英文 英語の文章の全体像を確認しよう

If you want to go to both the National Art Museum and the Metropolitan Museum, then I recommend that you go to the National Art Museum first. To get there, you can take the Number 12 bus or the Number 19 bus from the bus stop in front of the hotel. A bus only comes about once every 20 minutes, so you might have to wait for a few minutes.

You could also walk to the museum from here in about 15 minutes. To walk there, just go down this street and then you'll see a park on the left side. You could go through the park, but it might be easier to walk around the edge until you arrive at a big water fountain. In front of the water fountain, you'll see a stoplight. Cross the street and then turn right. If you walk for about 5 minutes, you'll see a big brown building, and that's the museum.

The Metropolitan Museum is only a few minutes from there, so after seeing the National Art Museum, you can ask someone for directions.

サンドイッチ文　意味のまとまりで区切って考えよう

▶ **If you want to go to**
もし行きたかったら

both the National Art Museum and the Metropolitan Museum,
国立美術館とメトロポリタン美術館の両方に

then I recommend that
私はおすすめしたい

you go to the National Art Museum first.
先に国立美術館へ行くことを

▶ **To get there,**
現地へ行くには

you can take the Number 12 bus or the Number 19 bus
12番か19番のバスで行ける

from the bus stop in front of the hotel.
ホテル正面のバス停から

▶ **A bus only comes about once every 20 minutes,**
バスは約20分おきに来る

so you might have to wait for a few minutes.[1]
数分待てばよい

▶ **You could also walk to the museum**[2] **from here**
ここから美術館へ歩いて行ける

in about 15 minutes.
約15分くらいで

▶ **To walk there,**
そこへ歩いて行くには

just go down this street
この通りを行くだけで

and then you'll see[3] **a park on the left side.**
左に公園があるのがわかるだろう

▶ **You could go through the park,**
公園を通り抜けられる

but it might be easier to walk around the edge
でも、端を回って行くほうが簡単かもしれない

until you arrive at a big water fountain.
大きな噴水のところまで

▶ **In front of the water fountain,**
噴水の前に

you'll see[3] **a stoplight.**
信号があるのが見えるだろう

▶ **Cross the street**
道を横断して

and then turn right.
それから右に曲がって

▶ If you walk for about 5 minutes,
5分くらい歩いたら
you'll see*3 a big brown building,
大きな茶色の建物が見えるだろう
and that's the museum.
それが美術館だ
▶ The Metropolitan Museum is only a few minutes from there,
メトロポリタン美術館へはそこからたった数分だ
so after seeing the National Art Museum,
だから、国立美術館を観た後は
you can ask someone for directions.
行き方を誰かに尋ねればよい

Keywords キーワード

once every XX minutes
XX分に一度

edge 端

water fountain 噴水式水飲み場

stoplight 信号

cross 横断する

direction 道順

Points ポイント

*1（P.64）
…so you might have to wait for a few minutes.

might（かもしれない）とhave to（しなければいけない）を一緒に使った、「～をしなければならないかもしれない」という表現。「～をしなければいけない」という意味を表す助動詞にはmustもありますが、助動詞は2つ続けて使うことができないので、have toを使います。

*2（P.64）
You could also walk to the museum…

You could…は「（あなた次第ですが）～をしたらどうですか」という控えめな提案。ここでは、一つ提案した後に「ほかの方法もあるよ」と言っているので、You could also…となっています。

*3（P.65、66）
…you'll see…

you'll see…（～が見えるでしょう）は、目印を教えるために道案内中に頻繁に使われる表現。日常会話では「いずれわかるよ」「本当だよ」といった意味で使われます。

日本語訳 文章全体としての訳し方を確認しよう

　国立美術館とメトロポリタン美術館に行きたいのでしたら、まず国立美術館へ先に行くことをおすすめします。そこへはホテル正面のバス停から12番か19番のバスで行けますよ。バスは約20分おきに出ているので、あと数分待てば来ますね。

　美術館へはここから歩いても、15分ほどで行けます。この通りを行くと、左に公園があります。その公園は通り抜けられますが、大きな噴水のところまで、端を回って行くほうがわかりやすいかもしれません。噴水の前に信号があります。そこを横断したら、右に曲がってください。5分ほど歩いたら、大きな茶色の建物が見えてきます。それが美術館です。

　メトロポリタン美術館へはそこから数分なので、国立美術館を観た後に、誰かに行き方を尋ねればいいですよ。

Sandwich method 11

駅：切符の買い方を教わる

**At the station -
Learning how to buy a ticket**

英文 英語の文章の全体像を確認しよう

　If this is your first time to visit Italy, then you might not be familiar with the train system here. So let me explain how it works.

　You can buy tickets from either one of the vending machines at the entrance, or you can stand in line and get your tickets at the window. However, sometimes the lines are quite long, so it's probably best to try to use the vending machines. You can pay for your tickets with cash, and one of the vending machines allows you to pay with a credit card. However, the vending machines don't always have the latest information. So if a vending machine says that a train is full, you still might be able to get a seat if you ask at the window.

　Once you get your tickets, there aren't any turnstiles or gate machines to go through. Instead, on the platforms, there's a little machine that you put your ticket in. This machine checks your ticket. Make sure you do this before you get on the train. If you forget and the ticket checker on the train catches you, then you might have to pay a large fine.

サンドイッチ文　意味のまとまりで区切って考えよう

▶ **If this is your first time to visit Italy,**
今回が初めてのイタリアの旅なら

then you might not be familiar
よくわからないかも

with the train system here.
電車のシステムが

▶ **So let me explain how it works.**
だから、どんな仕組みかを説明してあげる

▶ **You can buy tickets**
チケットは買える

<u>**from either one of the vending machines at the entrance,**</u>
いずれかの（方法の）うち、入口にある自動販売機の一つで、

<u>**or you can stand in line**</u>
もしくは、列に並んで

<u>**and get your tickets at the window.**</u>[*1]
窓口でチケットを受け取るか

▶ **However, sometimes the lines are quite long,**
でも、（窓口は）時々行列がすごく長くなる

so it's probably best to try
だから、試したほうがいいかもしれない

to use the vending machines.
自動販売機を使うことを

690

▶ You can can pay for your tickets with cash,
現金でチケット購入できる

and one of the vending machines allows you
一つの自動販売機では使える

to pay with a credit card.
支払いにクレジットカードが

▶ However,
とはいえ

the vending machines don't always have the latest information.
自動販売機はいつも最新情報があるわけではない

▶ So if a vending machine says that a train is full,
だから、機械が満席だと表示しても

you still might be able to get a seat
まだ席が取れるかもしれない

if you ask at the window.
窓口で聞いてみたら

▶ Once you get your tickets,
一旦チケットを手にしたら

there aren't any turnstiles or gate machines
(その先は) 回転式改札口もゲートもない

to go through.
通り抜ける

▶ Instead,
そのかわり

on the platforms,
プラットホームに

there's a little machine that you put your ticket in.
チケットを入れる小さな機械がある

▶ This machine checks your ticket.
その機械がチケットをチェックする

▶ Make sure you do this before you get on the train.[*2]
乗車前には必ずこれをして

▶ If you forget
もし忘れてしまい

and the ticket checker on the train catches you,
そのため列車内で係の人につかまったら

then you might have to pay a large fine.[*3]
多額の罰金を払わされるかもしれない

Keywords キーワード

familiar	よく知っている、精通している
vending machine	自動販売機
stand in line	行列に並ぶ
however	しかしながら

say	示す、書いてある
turnstile	回転式改札口
instead	代わりに
fine	罰金

Points ポイント

*1 (P.69)
…from either one of the vending machines… , or…at the window.
either A or B（AまたはBのどちらか）の慣用句を使った表現。Aが券売機、Bが窓口です。AとBは1語でも節でもOKですが、AとBは名詞と名詞、節と節のように対等のものを並べて。

*2 (P.71)
Make sure you do this before you get on the train.
Make sure that you do this...の接続詞thatが省略された一文。that以下の節で確かめるべき内容を説明します。会話ではthatを使うと堅苦しくなるので、接続詞が省略されがちです。

*3 (P.71)
If you forget and the ticket checker…catches you, then you…pay a large fine.
一文が長いので少しわかりにくいですが、大きな枠組みはif A, then B.（もしAならBである）というシンプルな構文。AはYou forget...catches you、Bはyou...pay a large fineです。

日本語訳　文章全体としての訳し方を確認しよう

　今回が初めてのイタリアでしたら、ここの電車のシステムがよくわからないかもしれませんね。では、どんな仕組みかご説明しましょう。
　入口の券売機か、窓口に並ぶか、いずれかの方法でチケットは購入できます。ただ、(窓口は)時々行列がすごく長くなるので、券売機を使うほうがいいかもしれません。(券売機は)現金払いと、一台の機械でクレジットカードが使えます。でも、券売機はいつも最新情報があるとは限りません。もし、座席に空きがないと機械が表示しても、窓口ではまだ購入できるかもしれませんん。
　チケットを購入したら、(その先に通り抜ける)回転式改札口もゲートもありません。そのかわり、プラットホームにチケットを入れる小さな機械があります。その機械が(あなたのチケットを)チェックします。乗車前には必ずこれをしてくださいね。もし忘れてしまったら、車内で係の人に捕まってしまい、多額の罰金を払わされるかもしれません。

Sandwich method 12

電車：車内アナウンスを聞く

**On the train -
Listening to the train announcements**

英文 英語の文章の全体像を確認しよう

The next stop is Camden Town on the High Barnet Line. Please be aware that the rearmost doors will not open. Passengers riding in the last car should use the other doors.

The doors are opening. Please get off the train in an orderly manner. Please mind the gap between the doors and the platform. Please move to the center of the car when boarding. The doors are closing. Please stand clear of the doors for your safety.

Thank you for using the London Underground. Please set your cell phone to silent mode and refrain from talking on the phone. Please offer your seat to elderly, pregnant, or unwell passengers. Please do not lean on the doors. If you see any suspicious items or persons, inform a member of the staff immediately. Do not enter the tracks. Smoking is prohibited in stations and trains.

| サンドイッチ文 | 意味のまとまりで区切って考えよう |

▶ **The next stop is Camden Town on the High Barnet Line.**
次はハイ・バーネット支線カムデンタウン駅

▶ <u>Please be aware that</u> the rearmost doors will not <u>open</u>.*1
いちばん後ろのドアは開かないので気をつけてください

▶ **Passengers riding in the last car**
最後部の車両の乗客は

should use the other doors.
前方のドアを使って

▶ **The doors are opening.**
ドアが開く

▶ **Please get off the train**
下車してください

in an orderly manner.
順序よく

▶ **Please mind the gap**
すき間に気をつけてください

between the doors and the platform.
ドアとホームの間の

▶ **Please move to the center of the car**
車内中ほどへ進んでください

when boarding.
乗車したら

▶ The doors are closing.
ドアが閉まる

▶ Please stand clear of the doors
ドアから離れてください

for your safety.
安全のために

▶ Thank you for using the London Underground.
ロンドン地下鉄にご乗車ありがとう

▶ Please set your cell phone to silent mode
携帯電話はマナーモードにしてください

and refrain from talking on the phone.*2
そして通話はしないように

▶ Please offer your seat to elderly, pregnant, or unwell passengers.
お年寄り、妊娠されている方、体調の悪いお客様に優先席をゆずってください

▶ Please do not lean on the doors.
ドアに寄りかからないでください

▶ If you see any suspicious items or persons,
もし、不審な物や人物を見かけたら

inform a member of the staff immediately.
すぐにスタッフに伝えて

▶ Do not enter the tracks.
線路内に入らないで

▶ Smoking is prohibited[*3] in stations and trains.
駅構内や車内では禁煙

Keywords キーワード

rearmost 最後部の	**boarding** 乗車、搭乗
in an orderly manner 整然と	**stand clear of...** 〜から離れて立つ
mind 注意する、用心する	**suspicious** 怪しい、疑わしい
gap すき間、間隙	**immediately** すぐに、早急に

Points ポイント

*1（P.74）
Please be aware that the rearmost doors will not open.
be aware that...は「〜のことに気づいて」という意味。続く語が名詞の場合はbe aware of...となり、Please be aware of the opening doors.（開くドアにご注意ください）に。

*2（P.75）
...refrain from talking on the phone.
refrain（控える）は、refrain from taking photographs（写真撮影を控える）など〈refrain from＋動名詞／名詞〉の形で公共の場で看板やアナウンスでよく利用されています。

*3（P.76）
Smoking is prohibited...
prohibit（禁じる）は法的な言及にもよく使われ、refrainとは違い厳しく禁じる表現。対義語の「許されている」は〈be動詞＋permitted〉や〈be動詞＋allowed〉です。

日本語訳　文章全体としての訳し方を確認しよう

　次はハイ・バーネット支線カムデンタウン駅です。いちばん後ろのドアは開きませんので、ご注意ください。最後部の車両にご乗車のお客様は、車両前方のドアをご利用ください。
　ドアが開きます。順序よく降車して（降りるお客様を先にお通し）ください。電車とホームの（間が大きく開いている場所があるので、乗り降りの際は）すき間にご注意ください。（ドア付近は混在しますので）ご乗車になりましたら、車内中ほどまでお進みください。ドアが閉まります。安全のために（危険ですので、）閉まるドアから離れてください。
　ロンドン地下鉄にご乗車ありがとうございます。携帯電話はマナーモードにして、通話はなさらないようお願いします。お年寄り、妊娠されている方、体調のすぐれないお客様に優先席をおゆずりください。ドアに寄りかからないでください。もし、不審なものや人物を見かけましたら、直ちに駅係員または乗務員にお知らせください。線路内には入らないでください。駅構内や車内は禁煙となっております。

Sandwich method 13

飛行機：
機内アナウンスを聞く

**On the airplane -
Listening to the inflight announcements**

> **英文** 英語の文章の全体像を確認しよう

　Ladies and gentlemen, welcome aboard Flight 259 from London to Milan. We are currently waiting for the okay to take off from the control tower. We apologize for the delay.

　We ask that you please remain seated with your seatbelt fastened and secure all baggage underneath your seat or in the overhead compartments. We also ask that you keep your seat and table tray in the upright position for take-off.

　There are six emergency exits on this aircraft, so please take a moment to locate the exit closest to you. Should the cabin experience sudden pressure loss, stay calm and listen for instructions from the cabin crew.

　Oxygen masks will drop down from above your seat. You'll need to place the mask over your mouth and nose, like this, and then pull the strap to tighten it. If you are traveling with children, please put your own mask on first, and then help your children.

　Please take a moment to review the safety card in the seat pocket in front of you. And, finally, we ask that you make sure that all carry-on luggage is stowed away safely during the flight.

サンドイッチ文 意味のまとまりで区切って考えよう

▶ **Ladies and gentlemen,**
皆さま

welcome aboard Flight 259 from London to Milan.
ロンドン発ミラノ行き259便にようこそ

▶ **We are currently waiting for the okay**
現在、我々は許可を待っている

to take off from the control tower.
管制塔からの離陸の（許可を）

▶ **We apologize for the delay.**
遅れに関してお詫びする

▶ **We ask that you please**[*1]
お願いします

remain seated with your seatbelt fastened
着席したままシートベルトをしめるよう

and secure all baggage underneath your seat
そして、座席の下にある手荷物すべての安全も確認するよう

or in the overhead compartments.
頭上の収納棚の中も

▶ **We also ask that you**
さらに、お願いします

keep your seat and table tray in the upright position
座席とテーブルを真っ直ぐに保つよう

for take-off.
離陸のため

▶ **There are six emergency exits on this aircraft,**
この飛行機には6つの非常口がある

so please take a moment
だから、時間を割いてください

to locate[*2] **the exit closest to you.**
いちばん近くの非常口の場所（の確認）に

▶ **Should the cabin experience sudden pressure loss,**[*3]
機内で急激な気圧低下のあった場合

stay calm and listen for instructions
落ち着いて指示を聞くように

from the cabin crew.
客室乗務員の

▶ **Oxygen masks will drop down from above your seat.**
酸素マスクは座席の上から落ちてくる

▶ **You'll need to place the mask over your mouth and nose,**
口と鼻にマスクをかぶせる必要がある

like this,
このように

and then pull the strap to tighten it.
そして、紐を引いてしめて

▶ **If you are traveling with children,**
もし子供と一緒に旅行をしているなら

please put your own mask on first,

最初にあなたがマスクをつけてください

and then help your children.

その後に子供を手伝って

▶ Please take a moment

時間を割いてください

to review the safety card

安全のしおりで復習する（時間を）

in the seat pocket in front of you.

前方の座席ポケットの中にある

▶ And, finally, we ask

最後に、お願いしたい

that you make sure that all carry-on luggage

機内持ち込み手荷物を確認してほしい

is stowed away safely during the flight.

飛行中無事に収納されている（ことを）

Keywords キーワード

currently	現在のところ	**calm**	落ち着いた
baggage	かばん	**tighten**	しっかり締める
*スーツケース、バッグなど全般		**luggage**	かばん
compartment	仕切り		*トランク、バッグなどの入れ物に入った荷物
locate	(〜の場所を) 見つける	**be stowed away**	(物を) しまう

Points ポイント

*1 (P.79)
We ask that you please...
ask that... (〜をお願いします) は決まり文句。thatに頼みたい内容を続けます。

*2 (P.80)
...take a moment to locate...
take a moment to...は、簡単にささっと済ませるのではなく「時間をとって〜する」「じっくり〜する」という意味。

*3 (P.80)
Should the cabin experience sudden pressure loss,
文の主語 (the cabin) と助動詞 (should) を倒置させて、ifを省略した仮定法。ifを使う場合はIf the cabin should experience sudden pressure lossとなります。このshouldは「万一のshould」と言われ、実際に起こる可能性は少ないと思う気持ちを表します。

日本語訳 文章全体としての訳し方を確認しよう

　皆さま、ロンドン発ミラノ行き259便をご利用いただき、ありがとうございます。現在、当機は、管制塔からの離陸許可を待っております。出発が遅れましたこと、お詫び申し上げます。
　着席のままシートベルトをおしめになり、座席の下また頭上の収納棚にある手荷物すべての安全をご確認ください。また、離陸のため、座席とテーブルを真っ直ぐになおすようお願いいたします。
　当機には6つの非常口があります。いちばん近くの非常口をご確認ください。機内で急激な気圧低下のあった場合は、落ち着いて客室乗務員の指示をお聞きください。
　酸素マスクが天井から下りてきます。このように、マスクを口と鼻にかぶせ、紐を引いて絞めてください。お子様がご一緒の場合、まずご自身がマスクを装着してから、お子様のマスクをおつけください。
　お座席前のポケットにある、安全のしおりをご確認 (読んでおいて) ください。最後に、機内持ち込み手荷物が飛行中 (無事に) 収納されていることをご確認ください。

Sandwich method 14

空港：
到着ロビーでアナウンスを聞く

**In the arrival lobby -
Listening to announcements**

英文 英語の文章の全体像を確認しよう

Welcome to the Atlanta International Airport. Due to the typhoon, several flights have been delayed or canceled. If you have a connecting flight, please speak to a member of the ground crew to get the latest information about your flight. If your connecting flight has been canceled, we will try to help you find another flight to your destination.

If you're going to be leaving the airport, you'll need to take the courtesy trolley to the International Arrivals Center. A trolley leaves every 15 minutes just outside of Exit A. No smoking is allowed in this part of the airport or on the trolleys. Smoking is permitted only in the designated smoking areas on the first and second floors of the International Arrivals Center.

Please proceed to the Immigrations and Customs Areas before going to the baggage claim area. All passengers arriving on international flights will need to go through the health screening station. Please let the health authorities know if you have experienced any high fever, sore throat, runny nose or dizziness during the last 48 hours.

> **サンドイッチ文** 意味のまとまりで区切って考えよう

▶ Welcome to the Atlanta International Airport.

アトランタ国際空港にようこそ

▶ <u>Due to the typhoon,</u>[*1]

台風のため

several flights have been delayed or canceled.

いくつかの便が遅延や欠航になった

▶ If you have a connecting flight,

もし、乗継ぎ便があるなら

please speak to a member of the ground crew

地上スタッフと話してください

to get the latest information

最新情報を得るため

about your flight.

あなたのフライトの

▶ If your connecting flight has been canceled,

もし、あなたの乗継ぎ便が欠航なら

we will try to help you

我々が手伝いをする

find another flight to your destination.

目的地までの代替便を探す

▶ If you're going to be leaving the airport,

もし空港から離れるなら

you'll need to take the courtesy trolley

トロリーバスに乗らなければならないだろう

to the International Arrivals Center.

国際線到着センターへ向かう

▶ A trolley leaves every 15 minutes

トロリーバスは15分おきに出ている

just outside of Exit A.

出口Aの外から

▶ No smoking is allowed[*2]

禁煙となっている

in this part of the airport

空港のこのエリアでは

or on the trolleys.[*3]

及びトロリーバスの中も

▶ Smoking is permitted

喫煙は許される

only in the designated smoking areas

指定された喫煙コーナーでのみ

on the first and second floors

1階もしくは2階の

of the International Arrivals Center.

国際線到着センターで

▶ Please proceed to the Immigrations and Customs Areas

入国審査と税関手続へ進んでください

before going to the baggage claim area.

手荷物引取所に行く前に

▶ All passengers arriving on international flights

国際便で到着したすべての乗客は

will need to go through the health screening station.

検診ステーションを通らなければならない

▶ Please let the health authorities know

保健当局に申し出てください

if you have experienced

（この後に説明するような）経験があったならば

any high fever, sore throat, runny nose or dizziness

発熱やのどの痛み、鼻水、めまいが

during the last 48 hours.

過去48時間の間に

Keywords キーワード

connecting flight	乗り継ぎ便	**be permitted**	許された
latest	最新の	**designated**	指定された
courtesy	優遇の	**proceed**	進む、前進する
be allowed	許された	**screening**	（ふるい分けの）検査
		during	（～の）間

Points ポイント

*1（P.84）
Due to the typhoon,
due to（～のせいで）は、残念な結果の原因に多く使われます。because ofよりかしこまった言い方。

*2（P.85）
No smoking is allowed…
No … is allowedで「～は許可されていない」、つまり「禁止」という意味に。

*3（P.85）
No smoking is allowed… or on the trolleys.
orは肯定文で使う場合は「AかBか（どちらか）」ですが、否定文の場合は「AもBも（どちらも）」。この場合は、主語がNo smokingと否定文になっているので「AもBも（どちらも）」。

日本語訳　文章全体としての訳し方を確認しよう

　アトランタ国際空港にようこそ。台風のため、遅延や欠航になった便がいくつかあります。乗り継ぎの方は、最新情報を地上スタッフにお尋ねください。お客様の乗継便が欠航でしたら、目的地までの代替便の手配をお手伝いいたします。

　空港から出られる方は、国際線到着センターへ向かうトロリーバスにご乗車ください。バスは出口A（の外）から15分おきに出ております。空港のこのエリア、及びトロリーバスの中は禁煙となっております。喫煙される方は、国際線到着センターの1階もしくは2階の喫煙コーナーでお願いします。

　手荷物引取所に行かれる前に、入国審査と税関手続へお進みください。国際便で到着されたすべてのお客様は、検診ステーションをお通りください。48時間以内に、発熱やのどの痛み、鼻水、めまいがあった方は、保健当局にお申し出ください。

Sandwich method **15**

タクシー：運転手と雑談する
In the taxi – Chatting with the driver

英文 英語の文章の全体像を確認しよう

You're staying at Central Hotel in the downtown area?

Of course I can take you there. It usually takes about 30 minutes to get there, but the roads are really crowded today, so it's going to take us a little longer. One of the major freeways is closed now for repair work, so all the other roads are a lot busier than usual. But I know a few shortcuts, so I think we should be able to get to your hotel by at least 2:30.

So, is this your first time visiting Los Angeles? It's quite a big city and it's really spread out, so it's not very easy to go between one place and another. Of course, we do have trains and buses, but not many people use public transportation in LA because it's not very convenient. Most people live far from the center of the city and work in the downtown area, so they have to commute quite far for their jobs. For this reason, most people travel by car.

Okay, we're just about at your hotel now. I'll drop you off at the entrance and help you get your bags out of the trunk.

サンドイッチ文 意味のまとまりで区切って考えよう

▸ You're staying at Central Hotel
セントラルホテルに泊まっているの？
in the downtown area?
ダウンタウンの

▸ Of course I can take you there.
もちろん、私があなたを連れて行ける

▸ It usually takes about 30 minutes to get there,
いつもそこまではだいたい30分で着く
but the roads are really crowded today,
でも今日は道がすごく混んでいる
so it's going to take us a little longer.
なので、少々時間がかかりそう

▸ One of the major freeways is closed now
今、主要道路の1本が閉鎖されている
for repair work,
修理中のために
so all the other roads are a lot busier than usual.
だから、どの道路もいつもより混んでいる

▸ But I know a few shortcuts,
でも近道が2、3ある
so I think we should be able to get to your hotel[*1]
だから、ホテルに着けると思う
by at least 2:30.
遅くとも2時30分には

▶ **So, is this your first time visiting Los Angeles?**
では、ロサンゼルスは初めて？

▶ **It's quite a big city**
かなり大都市で

and it's really spread out,
かなり広い

so it's not very easy to go
だから、移動が楽じゃない

between one place and another.
いろんなところに行くには

▶ **Of course, we do have trains and buses,**[*2]
もちろん電車とバスはある

but not many people use public transportation in LA
でも、LAに住んでいる人で公共交通機関を使う人は少ない

because it's not very convenient.
なぜなら、あまり便利ではないから

▶ **Most people live far from the center of the city**
ほとんどの人が、街の中心から離れたところに住んでいる

and work in the downtown area,
そしてダウンタウンで働いている

so they have to commute quite far
だから、かなり遠くから通勤をしなくてはならない

for their jobs.
職場へと

▶ For this reason, most people travel by car.
そんな理由で、ほとんどの人が車移動が多い

▶ Okay, we're just about at your hotel now.*3
オーケー、そろそろホテル到着だ

▶ I'll drop you off at the entrance
入口であなたを降ろそう

and help you get your bags out of the trunk.
トランクから荷物を取り出してあげる

Keywords キーワード

repair work	改修工事	commute	通勤する
than usual	いつもより	for this reason	そんなわけで
at least	少なくとも	travel	（遠距離を）移動する
be spread out	広がっている	drop (you) off	車から降ろす

Points ポイント

*1（P.89）
…we should be able to get to your hotel…

推量のshould（〜のはずだ）と可能のbe able to…（〜できる）を重ねて使うことで、「可能だろう」と強い確信を伝えることができます。

*2（P.90）
Of course, we do have trains and buses,

動詞の原形の前にdoを置くと、動詞の意味が強調できます。主語がheやsheなどの3人称の場合はdoesを。過去形の文を強調したい場合はdidを使います。

*3（P.91）
…we're just about to your hotel now.

〈be動詞＋about to…〉で「まさに〜しようとしている」。toの後にget toが省略されているので「まさに到着しようとしている」つまり「もう着く」という意味になります。almost there（そこまでもうちょっと）と言うことも。

日本語訳　文章全体としての訳し方を確認しよう

　ダウンタウンのセントラルホテルにお泊まりですね？
　はい、そちらまでお送りします。いつもですと30分くらいで着きますが、今日は道路がすごく混んでいるので、少々時間がかかるかもしれません。今、主要道路の1本が修理中で閉鎖されているため、どの道路もいつもより混んでいるんです。でも、2、3近道がありますので、ホテルには遅くとも2時30分には着くと思います。
　では、ロサンゼルスは初めてですか？　大都市でとても広いですから、いろいろなところに行くには移動が大変ですね。もちろん電車とバスはありますが、あまり便利ではないので、LAに住んでる人で公共交通機関を使う人は少ないです。ほとんどの人が郊外に住んでいて、ダウンタウンで働いているので、遠くから通勤しています。そのため、車移動が多いですね。
　はい、そろそろホテルに着きます。お客様を入口で降ろしてから、トランクからお荷物を出しますね。

Sandwich method 16

ホテル：チェックインする
At the hotel - Checking in

英文 英語の文章の全体像を確認しよう

Okay, we have your reservations. You asked for a single room, but all our single rooms are full. We can upgrade you to one of our larger rooms, if that's okay. The price is the same.

Here's your key. It's a card key, so slide it like a credit card to open the door. It sometimes doesn't work the first time, but just try it a couple of times and it should work. Your plan includes breakfast. Here's your voucher. Breakfast is available on the second floor restaurant from 7:30 to 10:00. You need to show this at the door.

Also, you can usually catch a taxi to go to the downtown area from here, but we also have a bus that leaves once an hour at the top of the hour. For example, 2:00, 3:00, 4:00, and so on. If you let someone at the front desk know you want to go somewhere, they'll tell the bus driver to wait for you.

Do you need anything or do you have any questions?

サンドイッチ文 意味のまとまりで区切って考えよう

▶ Okay, we have your reservations.
　はい、あなたの予約は入っている

▶ You asked for a single room,
　あなたはシングルルームが希望だった

but all our single rooms are full.
　でも、全室満室になってしまった

▶ We can upgrade you
　あなたはアップグレードできる

to one of our larger rooms,
　大きな部屋に

if that's okay.
　もしよければ

▶ The price is the same.
　料金は同じ

▶ Here's your key.*1
　キーをどうぞ

▶ It's a card key,
　それはカードキーです

so slide it like a credit card
　それを、クレジットカードのようにスライドする

to open the door.
　ドアを開けるために

▶ It sometimes doesn't work the first time,
　一度でうまくいかないこともある

but just try it a couple of times
でも、とにかく何回か試してみて

and it should work.
そうすればうまくいくはずだ

▶ Your plan includes breakfast.
あなたのプランは朝食がついている

▶ Here's your voucher.
これが引換券

▶ Breakfast is available
朝食は利用できる

on the second floor restaurant
2階のレストランで

from 7:30 to 10:00.
7時30分から10時まで

▶ You need to show this
あなたは、これを見せないとならない

at the door.
入口で

▶ Also, you can usually catch a taxi
それから、たいていタクシーがつかまる

to go to the downtown area from here,
ここからダウンタウンに行くのに

but we also have a bus
でも、バスもある

that leaves once an hour at the top of the hour.

1時間ごと、ちょうどの時刻に出る

▶ **For example, 2:00, 3:00, 4:00,**[*2] **and so on**[*3].

たとえば、2時ちょうど、3時ちょうど、4時ちょうどというように

▶ If you let someone at the front desk know

フロントデスクの誰かに知らせれば

you want to go somewhere,

どこか出かけたいと

they'll tell the bus driver

彼らがバスドライバーに伝えるだろう

to wait for you.

あなたを待つように

▶ Do you need anything

ほかに何か必要なものはある？

or do you have any questions?

または、知りたいことはある？

Keywords キーワード

upgrade　アップグレードする	available　利用できる、得られる
work　動く、作動する	once an hour　1時間に1回
include　含める	at the top of the hour
voucher　引換券	○時ちょうどに
	*時計の長針が12を指すとき

Points ポイント

*1 (P.94)
Here's your key.
hereは何かを手渡すときの「どうぞ」の表現。Here it is.やHere you are.（はい、どうぞ）としてよく使われます。カジュアルなシーンではHere you go.でもOK。

*2 (P.96)
For example, 2:00, 3:00, 4:00,
for example（たとえば）と前置きして直前の一文の補足情報を提供することで、at the top of the hourの意味を説明しています。具体例を挙げて説明する際に便利なテクニックです。

*3 (P.96)
...and so on.
時刻の羅列の後にくるand so onは、etc.のように「などなど」という意味。and so forthも同じような意味で、and so on and so forthと重ねて使うこともあります。

日本語訳　文章全体としての訳し方を確認しよう

　はい。ご予約は承っております。シングルルームがご希望のようでしたが、すべての（シングル）ルームが満室になってしまいました。もしよろしければ、大きなお部屋にアップグレードさせていただきます。（シングルルームと）同じお値段でご利用いただけます。
　（お部屋の）キーをどうぞ。そちらは、カードキーになっております。それを、クレジットカードのようにスライドしてドアを開けてください。一度で開かないこともありますが、何回か試していただければうまくいくと思います。このプランには朝食が含まれております。こちらの引換券をどうぞ。朝食は7時30分から10時までご利用いただけます。こちらを入口で（スタッフに）お見せください。
　また、こちらからダウンタウンへは、タクシーと、1時間ごと、ちょうどの時刻に発車いたします、ホテルのバスもご利用いただけます。（バスの発車時刻は）たとえば2時ちょうど、3時ちょうど、4時ちょうどなどです。どちらかにお出かけになりたい旨、フロントデスクにお知らせくだされば、バスに待機するよう連絡いたします。
　ほかに何かご入り用なもの、またはご質問はございませんか？

Sandwich method 17

ホテル：アクティビティについて聞く

At the hotel - Receiving information about available activities

> **英文** 英語の文章の全体像を確認しよう

My name is Linda Laurence, and I'm the concierge at the Mountain View Hotel. If there's anything I can do to make your stay more enjoyable, please let me know. I'd like to recommend a few activities that you might enjoy during your stay. The weather tomorrow is going to be sunny in the morning, but it may rain a little in the afternoon. In the morning, if you wake up early enough, you might want to go to the local farmers market. It's only two or three minutes from here, in the park in front of the train station. I recommend going to the Green River Museum in the afternoon. There you can learn about our local history and culture. But they also offer a lot of craft activities, so I'm sure your children would enjoy it.

If you choose to stay in the hotel instead of going out in the rain, you can enjoy the indoor swimming pool and gym on the 4th floor. They're open from 8:00 in the morning until 9:30 in the evening.

Again, please let me know if there's anything I can do to make your stay more enjoyable.

サンドイッチ文 意味のまとまりで区切って考えよう

▶ **My name is Linda Laurence,**
私はリンダ・ロレンス

and I'm the concierge at the Mountain View Hotel.[*1]
ここマウンテンビュー・ホテルのコンシェルジュです

▶ **If there's anything I can do**
もし私ができることがあれば

to make your stay more enjoyable,
あなたの滞在がより楽しくなるために

please let me know.
私に教えてください

▶ **I'd like to recommend a few activities**
おすすめの観光がいくつかある

that you might enjoy during your stay.
あなたが滞在中に楽しめる

▶ **The weather tomorrow**
明日の天気は

is going to be sunny in the morning,
朝のうちはとてもいい

but it may rain a little in the afternoon.
でも、午後からは少し雨が降るかもしれない

▶ **In the morning,**
朝

if you wake up early enough,
もし、充分早起きしたら

you might want to go to the local farmers market.[*2]
地元のファーマーズ・マーケットに行くのがいい

▶ It's only two or three minutes from here,
ここから2、3分で行ける

in the park in front of the train station.
駅前にある公園の

▶ I recommend going to the Green River Museum
グリーンリバー・ミュージアムに行くことを私はすすめる

in the afternoon.
午後は

▶ There you can learn about
そこでは知ることができる

our local history and culture.
この土地の歴史と文化を

▶ But they also offer
そこでは、(この後説明するものも) やっている

a lot of craft activities,
いろいろなワークショップを

so I'm sure your children would enjoy it.
だから子どもたちも楽しめるはずだ

▶ If you choose to stay in the hotel
ホテルにいるほうを選ぶなら

instead of going out in the rain,
雨の中を出かけるよりも

you can enjoy the indoor swimming pool and gym
室内プールとジムで楽しめる

on the 4th floor.
4階の

▶ They're open
そこは営業している

from 8:00 in the morning
朝8時から

until 9:30 in the evening.
夜9時30分まで

▶ <u>Again,</u> *3
では

please let me know
私に伝えてください

if there's anything I can do
もし、私にできることが何かあったら

to make your stay more enjoyable.
あなたの滞在がより楽しくなるように

Keywords キーワード

enjoyable	楽しめる
recommend	すすめる
activity	活動、娯楽、観光

early enough	充分早く
craft activity	ワークショップ
instead of...	〜の代わりに

Points ポイント

*1 (P.99)
...I'm the concierge at the Mountain View Hotel.
通常、職業名にはaをつけます。theを使うのは、職場に「1人しかいない」場合が主です。その仕事の責任者や、その日に限って1人しかいない場合もtheです。ここでaではなくthe conciergeと言っているのは「私が責任を持ってお客様に対応します」という意志を表しているからです。

*2 (P.100)
...you might want to go to the local farmers market.
might want toは「〜するといいでしょう」「〜したほうがいいでしょう」という意味。had betterやshouldのように上から目線にならない言い方なので、ビジネスシーンでも使えます。

*3 (P.101)
Again,
一度言ったことを思い出させるときに使う表現。感謝や謝罪の気持ちを強調するときにもよく使われ、「重ね重ね」や「何度もすみません」といった気持ちを伝えます。

日本語訳 文章全体としての訳し方を確認しよう

　マウンテンビュー・ホテルのコンシェルジュをしております、リンダ・ロレンスです。お客様のご滞在が楽しいものになるよう、何かございましたらどうぞお知らせください。
　滞在中お楽しみいただける、おすすめのアクティビティがいくつかございます。明日の天気は、朝のうちはとてもいいようですが、午後からは少しの雨が予想されます。早起きされたら、ファーマーズ・マーケットに行かれるとよいでしょう。ここから2、3分で行ける、駅前公園でやっています。午後はグリーンリバー・ミュージアムに行かれてはいかがでしょうか。この土地の歴史と文化を知ることができます。いろいろなワークショップをやっているので、お子様にも楽しんでいただけるかと思います。
　雨の中をお出かけになるよりホテルにいらっしゃるのがよろしければ、4階の室内プールとジムがいいでしょう。朝8時から夜9時30分まで営業しております。
　では、お客様のご滞在がより楽しくなりますよう、何かございましたらどうぞお知らせください。

Sandwich method 18

ホームステイ：
家族のルールを教わる

During a homestay -
Learning the house rules

英文 英語の文章の全体像を確認しよう

Hi, I'm Emma. This is my husband Evan, our daughter Helen, and our husky dog, Andy.

Your room is on the second floor. It's the corner room that faces south. There's a bed, a desk, and a closet, so make yourself at home.

If you would like me to wash any of your clothes, please give them to me in the evening, and I'll wash them with our laundry.

Feel free to use the kitchen. Please just wash any dishes you use and put them away. You can also use the refrigerator, but you should probably write your name on your food so we know it's yours.

Separate the garbage into combustibles and non-combustibles. Combustibles are taken out on Mondays and Wednesdays. Non-combustibles are only collected on Tuesdays, so don't forget.

We take the dog for a walk in the park every morning. It's really good exercise. You're welcome to come along.

You can also watch the TV in the living room or read the newspapers and magazines.

サンドイッチ文 意味のまとまりで区切って考えよう

▶ **Hi, I'm Emma.**
こんにちは。私はエマ

▶ **This is my husband Evan,**
こちらがダンナのエヴァン

our daughter Helen,
（そして）娘のヘレン

and our husky dog, Andy.
そして、ハスキー犬のアンディ

▶ **Your room is on the second floor.**
あなたの部屋は2階

▶ **It's the corner room**
それは角部屋だ

that faces south.
南向きの

▶ **There's a bed, a desk, and a closet,**
ベッドとデスクとクローゼットがある

so make yourself at home.
だから、自由に使って

▶ **If you would like me to wash**
もし私に洗濯してほしかったら

any of your clothes,[1]
あなたの服を

please give them to me in the evening,
夜に私にください

and I'll wash them
そうすれば、洗ってあげる

with our laundry.
私たちの洗濯物と一緒に

▶ Feel free to use the kitchen.
キッチンは自由に使っていい

▶ Please just wash any dishes you use
使ったお皿はちゃんと洗ってください

and put them away.
そして、片付けて

▶ You can also use the refrigerator,
冷蔵庫も自由に使っていい

but you should probably write your name on your food
でも、食品に名前を書いておいたほうがいい

 so we know it's yours.
そうすれば、それがあなたのだとわかる

▶ Separate the garbage
ゴミは分別して

into combustibles and non-combustibles.[*2]
燃えるものと燃えないものに

▶ Combustibles are taken out on Mondays and Wednesdays.
可燃ゴミは、毎週月曜と水曜に収集される

▶ **Non-combustibles are only collected on Tuesdays,**
不燃ゴミは火曜にだけ収集される
so don't forget.
だから、忘れないで

▶ **We take the dog for a walk in the park**
犬の散歩に近くの公園まで行く
every morning.
毎朝

▶ **It's really good exercise.**
それは、なかなかいい運動だ

▶ **You're welcome to come along.**
よかったら一緒にどうぞ

▶ **You can also watch the TV**
TVも（自由に）見ていい
in the living room
リビングルームの
or read the newspapers and magazines.
それに新聞や雑誌も読んで（いい）

Keywords キーワード

face （〜の方角に）向いている	refrigerator 冷蔵庫
make oneself at home くつろぐ	combustibles 可燃ゴミ
feel free to... 遠慮なく〜して	non-combustibles 不燃ゴミ
(Please) just... ちゃんと〜して	you're welcome to... どうぞ〜してください

Points ポイント

*1（P.104）
If you would like me to wash any of your clothes,

would like to...は、want to...（〜をしたい）をフォーマルにした表現。「（人）に〜をしてほしい」と言う場合は、この文のme to washように「人」がtoの前に入ります。

*2（P.105）
Separate the garbage into combustibles and non-combustibles.

separateは「離す」「分かれる」という単語で、〈separate XXX into A and B〉で「XXXをAとBに分ける」という意味に。〈separate A from B〉は「AからBを離す」という意味です。

日本語訳 文章全体としての訳し方を確認しよう

　こんにちは。私はエマよ。こちらは主人のエヴァン。そして娘のヘレンにハスキー犬のアンディ。
　あなたの部屋は2階の南向きの角部屋よ。ベッドもデスクもクローゼットもあるから、自由に使ってね。
　何か洗濯してほしい服があったら、夜にくれればうちのと一緒に洗ってあげるわ。
　キッチンは自由に使ってね。使ったお皿は洗って片付けておいてね。冷蔵庫も自由に使っていいわよ、でもあなたのだってわかるように、食品に名前を書いておいたほうがいいわね。
　ゴミは燃えるものと燃えないものに分別してね。ゴミの収集日は燃えるものは毎週月曜と水曜。燃えないものは火曜だけだから、忘れないでね。
　毎朝、犬の散歩に近くの公園まで行くの。いい運動になるわよ。よかったら一緒にどうぞ。
　リビングのTVも自由に見てね、新聞や雑誌もね。

Sandwich method 19

ホテル：
換金方法について教わる

At the hotel -
Learning how to exchange money

英文 英語の文章の全体像を確認しよう

Okay, it looks like everyone is here. So let me give you some basic information.

If you want to exchange money, you can ask at the hotel's front desk. However, the exchange rates aren't very good, and they also have high fees. If you can wait until tomorrow morning, I recommend going to one of the banks nearby during business hours.

The closest bank is about two minutes from the hotel. They close at 4:00, and they're not open on the weekends, so plan carefully. The exchange rates there are much better than the hotel's rates.

But if you want to get the best rate, you should use your credit card to get money from an ATM. Most of the ATMs in this country are available between 8:00 in the morning and 9:00 in the evening. There are ATMs located all throughout the city, but the closest one from here is on the left side of this street under a large blue sign.

Don't forget that some stores don't take credit cards, so you'll need to have a little cash. And it's also good to have some change for trains and buses.

> **サンドイッチ文**　意味のまとまりで区切って考えよう

▸ Okay, it looks like everyone is here.[1]
さて、全員ここにいるらしい

▸ So let me give you some basic information.
なので、基本的な情報を伝えよう

▸ If you want to exchange money,
もし換金したければ

you can ask at the hotel's front desk.
ホテルのフロントデスクでやってくれる

▸ However, the exchange rates aren't very good,
でも、換金レートはあまりよくない

and they also have high fees.
かつ、手数料も高い

▸ If you can wait until tomorrow morning,
もし、明朝まで待てるなら

I recommend going to one of the banks nearby
近くの銀行に行くのをすすめる

during business hours.
営業時間内に

▸ The closest bank
ここからいちばん近い銀行は

is about two minutes from the hotel.
ホテルからだいたい2分くらい

▸ They close at 4:00,
4時には閉まる

and they're not open on the weekends,
そして、週末は空いていない
so plan carefully.
だから、計画は慎重に立てて

▶ The exchange rates there
そこの（銀行の）換金レートは
are much better than the hotel's rates.
ホテルのレートよりずっといい

▶ But if you want to get the best rate,
でも、もしあなたがベストな換金レートを望むならば
you should use your credit card
クレジットカードを使うべきだ
to get money from an ATM.
ATMでお金を引き出すために

▶ Most of the ATMs in this country
この国のほとんどのATMが
are available
使えるのは
between 8:00 in the morning and 9:00 in the evening.
朝8時から夜9時まで

▶ There are ATMs located all throughout the city,[2]
町中至る所にATMがある

but the closest one from here
でも、ここからいちばん近いのは
is on the left side of this street
この通りの左側の
under a large blue sign.
大きな青い看板の下にある

▶ Don't forget that
忘れないように
some stores don't take credit cards,
クレジットカードを使えない店がいくつかあることを
<u>so</u> you'll need to have a little cash.*3
だから、現金も少しあったほうがいい

▶ And it's also good to have some change
それに小銭もいくらかあるといい
for trains and buses.
電車やバス用に

Keywords キーワード

exchange	両替する	business hours	営業時間
exchange rate	為替のレート	throughout	〜の至る所に
fee	手数料	closest one	一番近いもの、所
nearby	近くの	change	小銭

Points ポイント

*1（P.109）
...it looks like everyone is here.
it looks like...は直訳すると「〜のように見える」ですが、I think...のニュアンスを含むので、「見たところ全員がここにいるようだ」「皆さんお集りのようですね」という意味に。

*2（P.110）
There are ATMs located all throughout the city,
locatedはlocation（位置）の形容詞。多くの場合、後に前置詞を伴って場所を示す表現が続きます。小さい場所にはat、道路や広い場所にはon、国などの大きな場所にはinを使います。

*3（P.111）
...so you'll need to have a little cash.
単純未来を表すwillを使うことで、You need to...（あなたは〜する必要がある）と言っても命令口調に感じさせない、やや丁寧なニュアンスになります。

日本語訳 文章全体としての訳し方を確認しよう

　さて、皆さんお集りのようですね。では、基本的なことをお教えしましょう。
　換金したい場合は、ホテルのフロントデスクでやってくれます。ただし、換金レートはあまりよくありませんし、手数料も高いです。明朝まで待てるのでしたら、営業時間に近くの銀行に行くのがいいでしょう。
　ここからいちばん近い銀行は、ホテルからだいたい2分です。でも（営業時間）4時までで、週末も開いていないので、予定は慎重に立ててください。換金レートは、ホテルのよりずっといいですよ。
　でも、ベストなレートで換金したいのでしたら、クレジットカードを使ってATMで引き出すといいですよ。この国のほとんどのATMは、朝8時から夜9時までしか使えません。ATMは街中の至る所にありますが、ここからいちばん近いところ（ATM）は、この通りの左側の、大きな青い看板の下にあります。
　クレジットカードを使えないお店もいくつかあるので、少しは現金を持っているようにしてください。それに、電車やバス用に小銭もあったほうがいいですね。

Sandwich method 20

テレビ：天気予報を見る
On TV - Watching the weather report

英文　英語の文章の全体像を確認しよう

Now, here's the forecast for tomorrow. There's a band of clouds hanging over the West Coast right now. The weather will clear up for a short period as the clouds move down to the south tonight, but the clouds will probably move back up north tomorrow. The low-pressure system is expected to bring heavy rain showers to a large area tomorrow. Don't forget to take an umbrella when going out. Also, watch out for rising rivers and possible landslides when the rain starts pouring. Due to these unstable conditions, people doing water sports and people near the coast need to watch out for lightning. It will be hot again tomorrow, so if you're going to be active outside, you should be careful not to get heatstroke.

Now for the weekly forecast. The high-pressure system in the east will bring generally clear and hot days to the East Coast. The weather will gradually deteriorate toward the end of the week. Scattered showers in the west coast will continue until Friday, but then it should clear up on the weekend.

This is Sally Gomez reporting.

サンドイッチ文　意味のまとまりで区切って考えよう

▶ **Now, here's the forecast for tomorrow.**

次は、明日の天気予報

▶ **There's a band of clouds**

帯状の雲がある

hanging over the West Coast*1 right now.

現在、西海岸を覆うように

▶ **The weather will clear up for a short period**

天気は、しばらくの間は回復するだろう

as the clouds move down to the south tonight,

今夜、雲が南に下がるにつれて

but the clouds will probably move back up north tomorrow.

しかし、明日、雲は再び北上するだろう

▶ **The low-pressure system is expected**

低気圧から、予想される

to bring heavy rain showers

激しいにわか雨をもたらすことが

to a large area tomorrow.

明日は広い範囲に

▶ **Don't forget to take an umbrella when going out.*2**

外出の際は傘をお忘れなく

▶ **Also, watch out for rising rivers**

また、ご注意を。河川の増水と

and possible landslides
土砂災害に

when the rain starts pouring.
雨が激しく降り出したら

▶ Due to these unstable conditions,
不安定な天気なので

people doing water sports
マリンスポーツをする人

and people near the coast
また、海辺で過ごす人は

need to watch out for lightning.
カミナリに注意する必要がある

▶ It will be hot again tomorrow,
明日はまた暑くなるだろう

so if you're going to be active outside,
そのため、屋外で活動する予定があるならば

you should be careful
気をつけたほうがよい

not to get heatstroke.
熱中症にならないように

▶ Now for the weekly forecast.
次は、週間予報

▶ The high-pressure system in the east
東側にある高気圧により

will bring generally clear and hot days

おおむね晴れの暑い日々をもたらすだろう

to the East Coast.

東海岸に

▶ The weather will gradually deteriorate

天気は徐々に崩れる

toward the end of the week.

週末に向かって

▶ Scattered showers in the west coast

西海岸のにわか雨は

will continue until Friday,

金曜日まで続くだろう

but then it should clear up on the weekend.

しかし、週末は晴れる（だろう）

▶ This is Sally Gomez reporting.

サリー・ゴーメズがお伝えしました

Keywords キーワード

clear up	晴れ上がる
be expected...	～が予想される
landslide	土砂崩れ、地滑り
pour	ざあざあ降る
unstable	不安定な

heatstroke	熱中症
generally	ほとんど、だいたい
gradually	徐々に
deteriorate	悪化する
scattered shower	にわか雨

Points ポイント

*1（P.114）
There's a band of clouds hanging over the West Coast...

hanging over は「覆う」「張り出す」という意味。hanging over the West Coast（西海岸を覆う）がa band of clouds（帯状の雲）を修飾しています。

*2（P.114）
Don't forget to take an umbrella when going out.

丁寧に言うとDon't forget to take an umbrella with you...ですが、相手を特定する必要がないのでwith you は省略されています。

日本語訳　文章全体としての訳し方を確認しよう

　次は、明日の空模様です。現在、帯状の雲が西海岸全体を覆うようにかかっております。この雲は今夜一旦南下して天気は回復しますが、明日は再び北上する見込みです。この低気圧の影響で、明日は広い範囲で激しいにわか雨が予想されます。外出の際は傘をお忘れなく。また、激しい雨が降り出しましたら、河川の増水や土砂災害に十分ご注意ください。大気が不安定となりますので、マリンスポーツや海辺で過ごす予定の方は、カミナリにもご注意ください。明日も暑くなりますので、屋外で活動される方は熱中症にお気をつけください。

　続きまして、週間予報です。東側にある高気圧の影響で、東海岸はおおむね晴れ、暑い日が続くでしょう。週末に向かって徐々に天気が崩れます。西海岸は金曜日までぐずついた天候が続きますが、週末は晴れるでしょう。

　以上、サリー・ゴーメズがお伝えしました。

Sandwich method 21

テレビ：
スポーツニュースを見る

On TV - Watching the sports news

英文 英語の文章の全体像を確認しよう

　Ritter scored two goals as the Oklahoma Whirlwind beat the San Diego Busters 4 to 2 on Wednesday in Major League Soccer. San Diego saw its nine-game unbeaten run ended.
　Justin Woo made it 1 to 1 in the 29th minute with a left-footed shot after controlling a cross with his chest. Ritter's header from Ben Calderera's free kick gave the OK Whirlwind a 2 to 1 lead in the 39th. Four minutes later, Calderera converted a penalty after San Diego was called for a questionable foul.
　Ritter made it 4 to 1 in the opening minute of the second half when Jordan Sirven won the ball in San Diego territory and passed it to Ritter.
　Julian Peters was taken off injured 14 minutes into the first half. It appears he injured his hamstring. Coach Ryan Steward of the Busters told ABC, "It's not serious, but we'll have him sit out Tuesday's game as a precaution."

サンドイッチ文 意味のまとまりで区切って考えよう

▶ Ritter scored two goals
リッターが2ゴールを決めた

as the Oklahoma Whirlwind beat the San Diego Busters 4 to 2
オクラホマ・ウィルウィンドがサンディエゴ・バスターズを4対2で下した

on Wednesday in Major League Soccer.
水曜日に行われたメジャー・リーグ・サッカーの試合で

▶ San Diego saw its nine-game unbeaten run ended.[*1]
サンディエゴの連勝は9でストップした

▶ Justin Woo made it 1 to 1 in the 29th minute
29分に、ジャスティン・ウーが（ゴールを決めて）1対1の同点とした

with a left-footed shot
左足でシュートして得点したことによって

after controlling a cross with his chest.
クロスボールを胸でトラップした後

▶ Ritter's header from Ben Calderera's free kick
ベン・カルデレーラのフリーキックをヘディングしたリッター（のボール）が

gave the OK Whirlwind a 2 to 1 lead in the 39th.
39分に、OKウィルウィンドに2対1のリードをもたらした

▶ Four minutes later,
4分後

Calderera converted a penalty
カルデレーラがPKを決めた

after San Diego was called
サンディエゴが取られた後に

for a questionable foul.
判定に疑問が残るファールを

▶ Ritter made it 4 to 1
リッターが（得点を）決めて、4対1とした

in the opening minute of the second half
後半開始1分のときに

when Jordan Sirven won the ball in San Diego territory
ジョーダン・シルバンがサンディエゴ陣内でボールを奪った

and passed it to Ritter.
それをリッターにパスした

▶ Julian Peters was taken off injured[*2]
ジュリアン・ピーターズはケガのため交代させられた

14 minutes into the first half.
前半14分に

▶ It appears he injured his hamstring.[*3]
ももを痛めたとみられる

▶ Coach Ryan Steward of the Busters told ABC,
バスターズのライアン・スチュワード監督はABCの取材に答えた

"It's not serious,
深刻ではない

but we'll have him sit out Tuesday's game[*4]
しかし、彼には火曜日の試合を欠場してもらう

as a precaution."
大事をとって

Keywords キーワード

4 to 2 4対2	**convert a penalty** PKで得点する
unbeaten 負けたことのない	**questionable** 疑わしい
the 29th minute 29分目	**injured** 傷ついた
header ヘディング	**as a precaution** 用心のため

Points ポイント

*1（P.119）
San Diego saw its nine-game unbeaten run ended.
このseeは「経験する、目撃者となる」という意味なので、「9連勝が終わるという経験をした」というニュアンス。San Diego's nine-game unbeaten run（サンディエゴの9連勝）ではなく、チームを主語にすることで、目の前でそれが起きた悔しさが込められています。

*2（P.120）
Julian Peters was taken off injured…
スポーツの試合では〈be動詞＋taken off〉で「交代させられる」という意味に。

*3（P.120）
It appears he injured his hamstring.
appearは「〜のように見える、思われる」。そのため「彼はももを傷めたらしい」となります。

*4（P.121）
…we'll have him sit out Tuesday's game…
sit outは「参加せず」なので、「我々は火曜日の試合に彼を欠場させる」となります。

日本語訳　文章全体としての訳し方を確認しよう

　メジャー・リーグ・サッカーは、水曜日、リッターが2ゴールを決めるなどして、オクラホマ・ウィルウィンドがサンディエゴ・バスターズを4対2で下した。サンディエゴの連勝は9でストップした。

　29分にジャスティン・ウーがクロスボールを胸でトラップした後、左足で押し込み同点とした。39分、ベン・カルデレラーラのフリーキックからリッターがヘディングで決めて2対1とリードを奪った。4分後にはサンディエゴが判定に疑問が残るファールを取られ、カルデレラーラがPKを決めた。

　後半開始1分、ジョーダン・シルバンがサンディエゴ陣内でボールを奪い、シルバンからのパスをリッターが決めて、4対1とした。

　ジュリアン・ピーターズは前半14分に負傷交代。ももを痛めたとみられている。バスターズのライアン・スチュワード監督はABCの取材に対し、「深刻ではないものの、大事をとって火曜日の試合を欠場させる」と明かした。

Sandwich method 22

テレビ：料理番組を見る
On TV - Watching a cooking show

英文 英語の文章の全体像を確認しよう

Hello, everyone! Let me show you a spicy chicken dish. If you're thinking, "Jerk Chicken," you're spot on! So today let's make a simple Jamaican hot chicken dish!

Salt and pepper all of the chicken meat and melt butter in a hot frying pan. Then, put the drumsticks into the pan. Next, put in the thigh meat with the skin facing up. Now, spread this minced garlic over the chicken, slice half an onion and add it to the chicken. After that, add bell peppers. You can cut them to any size you like.

Now we need to give the chicken its Jamaican flavor. We'll be using habanero peppers. After you select the peppers you want and grind them up, add them to the pan. Sprinkle grated nutmeg and thyme over it and cook well. Once the chicken has browned, set it aside, and put the remaining vegetables into your blender. And blend away!

Put your chicken back in the frying pan, add the white wine and cover it with the lid. Add your sauce and simmer for 20 minutes. Put your finished chicken on a dish and sprinkle it with chopped parsley, add a squeeze of lime and you're done!

サンドイッチ文 意味のまとまりで区切って考えよう

▶ Hello, everyone!

皆さん、こんにちは！

▶ Let me show you a spicy chicken dish.

辛いチキン料理を紹介させて

▶ If you're thinking, "Jerk Chicken,"

すぐに「ジャークチキン」が浮かんだとしたら

you're spot on!*1

あなたはすごい！

▶ So today let's make

だから今日は作ろう

a simple Jamaican hot chicken dish!

簡単なジャマイカ風ピリ辛チキンを

▶ Salt and pepper all of the chicken meat

全部の鶏肉に塩コショウをしたら

and melt butter in a hot frying pan.

熱したフライパンに、溶かしバターを入れて

▶ Then, put the drumsticks into the pan.

その中に鶏の脚を入れる

▶ Next, put in the thigh meat with the skin facing up.

次はモモ肉を、皮が上になるように入れる

▶ Now, spread this minced garlic over the chicken,

さて、ここで刻んだガーリックを鶏肉全体にかけて

slice half an onion and add it to the chicken.

半分に切った玉ねぎをスライスして、鶏肉に加える

▶ After that, add bell peppers.
次に入れるのは、ピーマン

▶ You can cut them to any size you like.
大きさはお好みでOK

▶ Now we need to give the chicken its Jamaican flavor.
では、鶏肉をジャマイカ風にしよう

▶ We'll be using habanero peppers.
ハバネロを使おう

▶ After you select the peppers you want
使うハバネロを選んだら

and grind them up,
それをすりつぶして

add them to the pan.
フライパンの中に投入

▶ Sprinkle grated nutmeg and thyme over it
それから、ひいたナツメグとタイムも振りかけて

and cook well.
よく焼く

▶ Once the chicken has browned,
鶏肉がキツネ色になったら

set it aside,[*2]
取り出して

and put the remaining vegetables into your blender.
フライパンに残った野菜を、ブレンダーに入れる

▶ **And <u>blend away!</u>**[*3]

そして、スイッチオン！

▶ **Put your chicken back in the frying pan,**

鶏肉をフライパンに戻し

add the white wine and cover it with the lid.

白ワインを入れて蓋をする

▶ **Add your sauce**

ソースを鶏肉にかけ

and simmer for 20 minutes.

20分煮込む

▶ **Put your finished chicken on a dish**

できた鶏肉を皿に取り出して

and sprinkle it with chopped parsley,

刻みパセリを振りかけ

add a squeeze of lime

ライムを絞って

and you're done!

できあがり！

Keywords キーワード

drumstick	鶏の脚
thigh meat	もも肉
facing up	上に向けて
minced	みじん切りの
bell pepper	ピーマン

grind	つぶす
sprinkle	撒く、振りかける
grated	すりおろした
simmer	煮る
chopped	刻んだ

Points ポイント

*1（P.124）
…you're spot on!
「そのとおり！」「的を得ている！」「ビンゴ！」というニュアンスの表現。

*2（P.125）
Once the chicken has browned, set it aside,
onceは「～したら、いったん……して」と、条件を表す接続詞。ここでは「鶏肉がこんがり」してきたら、いったん「取り出して」と、後ろに続く一文につなげています。

*3（P.126）
…blend away!
walk away（立ち去る）、stay away（離れている）など、離れる動作を表すときにawayが使われます。ここではブレンダーをオンにしながら次の作業に移るイメージ。

日本語訳　文章全体としての訳し方を確認しよう

　皆さん、こんにちは！　今日は、辛いチキン料理をご紹介しましょう。すぐに「ジャークチキン」を思い浮かべた人、あなたはいいセンスしてますね！　では、今日は「簡単ジャマイカ風ピリ辛チキン」を作りましょう！

　鶏肉に塩コショウをしたら、熱したフライパンに溶かしバターを入れます。その中に鶏の脚を入れていきます。次はモモ肉を、皮が上になるように入れます。さて、ここで刻んだガーリックを鶏肉全体にかけて、玉ねぎ半分をスライスして、鶏肉に加えてください。次に入れるのは、ピーマンです。大きさはお好みで。

　さて、ここから、鶏肉がジャマイカ風になるポイントです。ハバネロを使います。使うハバネロを選んだら、すりつぶして、フライパンの中に入れます。そして、すりおろしたナツメグとタイムを振りかけて、よく焼きます。鶏肉がキツネ色になったら、一旦（皿に）取り出し、フライパンに残った野菜を、ブレンダーに入れてください。そして、スイッチオン！

　鶏肉をフライパンに戻し、白ワインを入れて蓋をします。ソースを鶏肉にかけ、20分煮込みます。できた鶏肉を皿に盛り付けたら、刻みパセリを振りかけ、ライムを絞ってできあがり！

Sandwich method 23

テレビ：通販番組を見る
On TV - Watching an infomercial

英文 英語の文章の全体像を確認しよう

Hello, everyone! Let me tell you today about a new product called Mega Slim Magic Pants from the makers of Slim Magic, the magical pants that have helped over six million women look slimmer.

Now the maker of Slim Magic has provided us with only 10,000 of their new and improved pants. While stocks last, you can get the Mega Slim Magic Pants in beige, black, or pink.

If you place an order within 30 minutes after seeing this infomercial, you will receive a free laundry net of the same color as your order! Isn't that a great deal? Don't miss out on this great opportunity!

Oh, wait! There's more! Order two in different colors and you will get free shipping and handling!

If you aren't satisfied, just return it! We'll give you your money back. Call right away!

Oh! We are getting flooded with phone calls! I apologize to those who can't get through to an operator right now. Our operators are frantically answering all of your calls. Don't give up and keep calling us!

サンドイッチ文 意味のまとまりで区切って考えよう

▶ Hello, everyone!
こんにちは、皆さん！

▶ Let me tell you today
今日は紹介させて

about a new product called Mega Slim Magic Pants
メガスリムマジックパンツという新商品について

from the makers of Slim Magic,
スリムマジックを作ったメーカーの

the magical pants
あの魔法のパンツ

that have helped over six million women look slimmer.
600万人の女性をスリムに変身させた

▶ Now the maker of Slim Magic
今回は、スリムマジックのメーカーが

has provided us with only 10,000
私たちのために、1万枚だけ確保した

of their new and improved pants.
この新しく改良された商品を

▶ <u>While stocks last,</u>*1
在庫がある

you can get the Mega Slim Magic Pants
入手できるメガスリムマジックパンツは

in beige, black, or pink.
ベージュ、ブラック、ピンク

▶ **If you place an order within 30 minutes**
30分以内に注文を確定すると

after seeing this infomercial,
この番組終了後

you will receive a free laundry net
無料で洗濯ネットが付いてくる！

of the same color as your order!
注文した下着と同色の

▶ **Isn't that a great deal?**
お得でしょう？

▶ **Don't miss out on this great opportunity!**[2]
この機会を見逃さずに！

▶ **Oh, wait! There's more!**
あ、ちょっと待って！　さらにさらに！

▶ **Order two in different colors**
色違いで2つ注文すると

and you will get free shipping and handling!
送料・手数料が無料になる！

▶ **If you aren't satisfied,**
もし、商品が気に入らなかったら

just return it!
返品すればいい！

- **We'll give you your money back.**
  支払額を返金する
- **Call right away!**
  今すぐ電話して!
- **Oh! We are getting flooded with phone calls!**
  おお! 電話が混み合ってきた!
- **I apologize to those**
  (該当する方に) 謝ります

  who can't get through to an operator right now.[3]
  今、なかなかオペレーターにつながらない方に
- **Our operators are frantically answering**
  オペレーターが必死で対応している

  all of your calls.
  あなたからの電話を
- **Don't give up and keep calling us!**
  あきらめず、繰り返し電話して!

Keywords キーワード

provide	供給する、提供する
improved	改良された
infomercial	インフォマーシャル
great deal	お得な買い物

opportunity	機会
shipping	配送
handling	出荷
get flooded	殺到する
frantically	必死になって

Points ポイント

*1（P.129）
While stocks last,
stock（在庫が）last（持続する）while（〜なかぎり）という意味なので、「今在庫があるものは」つまり「取りそろえているものは〜」というニュアンスになります。

*2（P.130）
Don't miss out on this great opportunity!
miss out on...で「〜（という好機）を見逃す」。Don't miss...（〜を見逃すな）もよく使われますが、miss out on...のほうが意識的にそうするというニュアンスが含まれています。

*3（P.131）
I apologize to those who can't get through to an operator right now.
関係代名詞whoの先行詞としてcan't以降の節がthose（people）を説明しています。

日本語訳 文章全体としての訳し方を確認しよう

　皆さま、こんにちは！　今日は、600万人の女性をスリムに変身させた、あの魔法のパンツ、スリムマジックを作ったメーカーの新商品、メガスリムマジックパンツをご紹介しちゃいます。
　今回はこのバージョンアップした商品をメーカー様から1万枚確保させていただきました！　取りそろえているもの（メガスリムマジックパンツのカラー）は、ベージュ、ブラック、ピンクです。
　この番組終了後、30分以内にご注文されると無料で下着と同色の洗濯ネットが付いてきます！　お得でしょう？　この機会を、どうぞお見逃しなく！
　あ、ちょっとお待ちください！　さらに、さらに！　色違いで2枚ご注文いただいた方に限り、送料・手数料が無料になります！
　万が一、商品が気に入らなかった場合は返品してください。お支払い金額をお返しします。今すぐお電話を！
　あ、電話が混み合ってきているようです！　なかなかオペレーターにつながらない方、申し訳ございません。オペレーターが必死で皆さまのお電話に対応させていただいております。あきらめないで、繰り返しお電話ください！

学習記録

「英語サンドイッチメソッド」は続けることが大切。
理解度や気づいたことなどを記録しておくと、学習成果が
ひとめでわかり、モチベーションアップに役立ちます。

例

タイトル	日にち	理解度	メモ
		65%	聞いていて違和感があるが、英語の意味はなんとなくわかった。

- CDを聞いてどれだけ理解できたか「%」で表します。
- 気づいた点や感想などをメモしておきましょう。

タイトル	日にち	理解度	メモ
Sandwich method 01	/	%	
Sandwich method 02	/	%	
Sandwich method 03	/	%	
Sandwich method 04	/	%	
Sandwich method 05	/	%	
Sandwich method 06	/	%	

タイトル	日にち	理解度	メモ
Sandwich method 07	/	％	
Sandwich method 08	/	％	
Sandwich method 09	/	％	
Sandwich method 10	/	％	
Sandwich method 11	/	％	
Sandwich method 12	/	％	
Sandwich method 13	/	％	
Sandwich method 14	/	％	
Sandwich method 15	/	％	

タイトル	日にち	理解度	メモ
Sandwich method 16	/	%	
Sandwich method 17	/	%	
Sandwich method 18	/	%	
Sandwich method 19	/	%	
Sandwich method 20	/	%	
Sandwich method 21	/	%	
Sandwich method 22	/	%	
Sandwich method 23	/	%	

英語サンドイッチメソッド
日常会話編
聞くだけ！
英語を話す力を
身につける
CDブック

発行日　2015年9月2日　第1刷
発行日　2017年12月12日　第20刷

著者	デイビッド・セイン

本書プロジェクトチーム

編集統括	柿内尚文
編集担当	舘瑞恵
ナレーション	Esther Thirimu、小林奈々子
デザイン	細山田光宣＋千本聡（細山田デザイン事務所）
イラスト	フクイヒロシ、中野きゆ美
編集協力	有坂ヨーコ（A to Z）、泊久代
校正	中山祐子、Richard Mort
CD制作	財団法人 英語教育協議会（ELEC）
営業統括	丸山敏生
営業担当	熊切絵理
営業	増尾友裕、石井耕平、戸田友里恵、甲斐萌里、大原桂子、綱脇愛、川西花苗、寺内未来子、櫻井恵子、吉村寿美子、田邊曜子、矢橋寛子、大村かおり、高垣真美、高垣知子、柏原由美、菊山清佳
プロモーション	山田美恵、浦野稚加
編集	小林英史、栗田亘、辺土名悟、村上芳子、加藤紳一郎、中村悟志、堀田孝之、及川和彦
編集総務	千田真由、髙山紗耶子、高橋美幸
メディア開発	池田剛
講演・マネジメント事業	斎藤和佳、高間裕子
マネジメント	坂下毅
発行人	高橋克佳

発行所　株式会社アスコム

〒105-0003
東京都港区西新橋2-23-1　3東洋海事ビル
編集部　TEL：03-5425-6627
営業部　TEL：03-5425-6626　FAX：03-5425-6770

印刷・製本　株式会社廣済堂

© A to Z Co., LTD　株式会社アスコム
Printed in Japan ISBN 978-4-7762-0885-3

本書は著作権上の保護を受けています。本書の一部あるいは全部について、株式会社アスコムから文書による許諾を得ずに、いかなる方法によっても無断で複写することは禁じられています。

落丁本、乱丁本は、お手数ですが小社営業部までお送りください。送料小社負担によりお取り替えいたします。定価はカバーに表示しています。